Mistakes in Academic Library Management

Grievous Errors and How to Avoid Them

Edited by
Jack E. Fritts Jr.

THE SCARECROW PRESS, INC.
Lanham • Toronto • Plymouth, UK
2009

Published by Scarecrow Press, Inc.
A wholly owned subsidiary of The Rowman & Littlefield Publishing Group, Inc.
4501 Forbes Boulevard, Suite 200, Lanham, Maryland 20706
http://www.scarecrowpress.com

Estover Road, Plymouth PL6 7PY, United Kingdom

British Library Cataloguing in Publication Information Available

Library of Congress Cataloging-in-Publication Data

Mistakes in academic library management : grievous errors and how to avoid
them / edited by Jack E. Fritts Jr.
    p. cm.
    Includes bibliographical references and index.
    ISBN 978-0-8108-6744-4 (alk. paper) — ISBN 978-0-8108-6745-1 (electronic)
    1. Academic libraries—Administration. 2. Academic libraries—United States—
Administration—Case studies. I. Fritts, Jack E., 1950–
Z675.U5M557 2009
025.1'977—dc22   2009016939

♾ ™ The paper used in this publication meets the minimum requirements of
American National Standard for Information Sciences—Permanence of Paper for
Printed Library Materials, ANSI/NISO Z39.48-1992.

Printed in the United States of America

Connie Costantino (1949–2009) was a true renaissance librarian. She worked in and directed school, public, and academic libraries throughout her long career. From 2003 to 2008 she was a lecturer at the San Jose State University School of Library Science, where she taught courses on topics such as library management. In her constant quest to provide the best type of library to her users, Connie continued to learn, seek expert advice, and lead by example, always with a smile on her face. She will be missed.

Contents

Introduction

Mistakes—we've all made them. Sometimes we commit minor errors like forgetting a name or missing an appointment. Sometimes we manage great big monstrous crashes that are career or life or relationship threatening. It's part of being human. Humans make mistakes. Managers are human; therefore managers make mistakes. I am sure many of you can find faults with this logic, but bear with me as I proceed.

In this book, several contributors take the plunge into the world of managerial mistakes. The focus is on academic library managers and the mistakes that occur within the academic library or campus boundaries, although the areas discussed are not the sole province of academic libraries or academic library managers. The topics presented will resonate with any library manager to some degree. This is not to suggest that only library managers make mistakes, but to bring to your attention some potential pitfalls and to offer suggestions for avoidance.

The ten chapters that follow look at some of the areas that academic library managers must encounter daily. Each chapter presents a tactical error of one sort or another and then discusses ramifications of the error and suggests ways of avoiding the mistake yourself. That is the real purpose of this book—to offer ideas and suggestions to help others avoid the snares some of us have already fallen into. The contributors come from a range of backgrounds and experiences, and each selected a specific area of focus for this book.

The managerial areas covered include staffing, communication, supervision, technology, and change. We also offer you a look at campus politics from both sides of the fence, through the writings of a library administrator and an academic vice president. I think you will find that the common thread running through these episodes is communication. We can make things work right or we can cause them to crash catastrophically through our communication skills. This book is designed to help all of us avoid the pitfalls that lie in wait for us as managers and administrators. I leave you with a quote from Franklin Delano Roosevelt (1882–1945), U.S. president (*FDR Speaks: Authorized Edition of Speeches, 1933–1945* [recordings of Franklin Roosevelt's public addresses], side 12, fourth inaugural address [January 20, 1945], ed. Henry Steele Commager, introduction by Eleanor Roosevelt, Washington Records, Inc., 1960):

> We shall make mistakes, but they must never be mistakes which result from faintness of heart or abandonment of moral principles. I remember that my old school master Dr. Peabody said in days that seemed to us then to be secure and untroubled, he said things in life will not always run smoothly, sometimes we will be rising toward the heights and all will seem to reverse itself and start downward. The great thing to remember is that the trend of civilization itself is forever upward.

1

Keeping Your Library on the Right (Correct) Side of Campus Politics

Thomas E. Abbott

It's the middle of February; spring semester final enrollments have been posted, and your state-supported institution is again facing its semiregular budget crisis. Leadership is looking for ways to cover a shortfall in tuition revenue before the end of the fiscal year. Once again, the vice president tells the library director that he or she has to find $40,000 to help solve the problem. In a side comment, the vice president indicates she has noticed in her budget summary that the library is one of the departments on campus that has more "operational" funds than it has salaries. The vice president reminds the library director that the academic departments have most of their money in faculty salaries, and the physical plant has just had to deal with an unbudgeted spike in heating fuel and electricity costs. The *coup de grâce*, however, is a comment by the chief financial officer about how he never really understood why the library couldn't just go a year without buying so many books.

This scenario is played out each year in academic institutions, small and large, public and private—only the players are different. Budget crises have been happening in public and private institutions at all levels for as long as they have existed. Publicly supported college and university libraries struggle to keep up with growing costs of services, especially when other commitments continue to escalate. In Maine, funding for the state's public higher education system has been flat for the last several years in my experience, resulting in reductions in services and increased tuition for students. As a result of this long-term problem, the University of Maine system has had to fight each year to avoid losses in reputation, enrollments, and the ability to attract and keep strong faculty members. At some point, budget crises trickle down to every library.

1

Certainly, a library director can't prevent budget crises from happening, nor can he or she expect never to have to pitch in to cover lower-than-expected revenues. That is one reality of administration. The expectations from above are that department heads must do the best they can with the money authorized for them. This perspective or difficult "reality" is not the same held by those in the libraries and on the front lines, where they witness daily pent-up demand for services, worn-out buildings, and growing interest in and demand for new technologies.

It is a well-known maxim that most library directors and their staff members don't work in libraries for the money. Most care deeply about their work, the community they serve, and the services they provide. This is often in contrast to the way libraries tend to be perceived within the echelon of senior decision makers. Often the first question university librarians hear from their staff when a new dean or vice president is hired is, "Is he or she a library supporter?" It seems a bit strange that a library's future existence might hang in the balance of this one question, but it really happens. This chapter will attempt to arm librarians with a few cognitive tools and strategies to help move the question of library support back under the library's control.

Despite strong administrative skills, advanced degrees, and years of experience on the part of directors and staff, libraries still often end up like the art and music programs in grade schools at the time of budget cuts: libraries find they have less support than for the hiring of faculty members for the classrooms, paying the oil bill, fixing the football field, or upgrading the computer lab.

Cynical replies to the library director's argument that the library needs more funding to keep up with technologies and services might sound like this: "You can't be all things to all people," or "They [citizens] voted for a tax reduction, and we have to make the tough decisions," or even "If you really want to be seen as a team player, you need to work with me here."

Anyone who's been in the library management business for any period of time will tell you there is no easy fix to the multiple problems described above. There are, however, some strategies that can be shared with staff and put in place that will better position the library at the time of budget crises and, more importantly, create a library-supportive environment on the campus.

THE CUSTOMER IS JOB ONE

With a nod to the Ford Motor Company in the title of this section, all libraries must include exceptional customer service in their strategic plan, with benchmarks that increase the depth of understanding and practice among staff for the three to five years of the plan—and educate all employees about its importance. Most libraries understand that good customer service is important and may have even held workshops on the topic. There is, however, no end to the need to keep visible the "excellent customer service" mantra for all staff and patrons to see, including the many student workers who come and go. Customer service is generally understood by organizational leaders, but getting it to happen all the time is not easy. If the library can regularly treat patrons with grace and friendliness and generally satisfy their needs, these patrons will become among its strongest allies. If the library staff can treat college administrators and academic leaders with exceptional service each and every time one calls or walks into the library, those leaders will leave with good feelings and may well remember them when considering how the next round of budget cuts will be shared.

What is excellent customer service? That is really for the library director and staff to decide as a team. There are plenty of useful and current guidelines on the web and from industry. Find and refine a version, present it to the staff or a staff subcommittee at a large library, and talk about excellent customer service as a strategy for gaining and maintaining library support—the necessary steps go beyond just satisfying customers on the day they are there. Set benchmarks each summer for the next five years, and measure, chart, and post the progress. Involving a supportive and well-connected support staff member from the dean's office wouldn't hurt either. Many major corporations post their mission statement for the public to see and to remind employees—not a bad idea!

Bottom line: Name the goal of excellent customer service, define it, post it, gain support from all staff to pursue it, implement the plan with necessary training and support, and then measure your results. Hint: One of your measures of success should be how well your institution's leadership responds to the changes.

LIBRARY VISIBILITY

Effective advertising and marketing requires a great deal of money. Why? Because it takes time to implant or change an image or idea in viewers' minds so they will buy the product or service. How many libraries spend 30 percent of their budget on marketing and promotion to make sure their customers know what the library is and does?

This version of promoting visibility of the library is about making sure your library gets a fair shake at the next round of internal university budget or planning decisions. The director should assume that campus decision makers already have a perception of the library based on their life experiences, and should expect that some of them remember unsatisfactory experiences more than good ones. Assuming you have to change or at least stabilize perceptions held by VIPs in the provost's, CFO's, or dean's office is where one should begin.

First steps include establishing an internal marketing and promotional strategy as part of the library's five-year strategic plan. If strategic planning is a new concept, help is available online for developing strategic plans, benchmarks, and assessment devices. Engage the entire staff and, as far as possible, members of the campus leadership in creating the strategic plan. A completed strategic plan is a valuable tool for guiding your growth, for helping focus staff, and for identifying results that can be shared with decision makers. Visualize saying this to your boss: "We know what we are supposed to do, we are doing it to 90 percent satisfaction of our customers, and we are working on the last 10 percent." Many departments aren't as organized or focused as your library can be. Not being organized with a strategic plan is a vulnerable spot to be in. If you do have assessment results from your plan, you will be ready to explain what you are doing and what you plan to do next. Engaging the institutional decision makers to assist the library in strategic planning can help forge positive and collaborative linkages for the library. Such collaboration can even provide an opportunity for the library to take a leadership role in planning and assessment for other, less organized departments—another place to build allies and visibility.

Conducting regular surveys about the effectiveness of library services is a great way to educate community members on what the library does and expects of itself. The survey itself is an educational/visibility opportunity. While participants take the library survey, they are also learning and ideally beginning to value more what the library cares about—like reading the library's mission statement on the wall of the reading room.

Bottom line: Everyone on campus should know what the library is about. Today a library has to be much more than a large space filled with resources, some of which are out of date and not being used. In most libraries, especially those supporting undergraduate students, make sure your primary focus is online resources, which should be paramount in your new image. If your library is still spending more on books than electronic resources, think again. Take advantage of any and all marketing funds and ideas—piggyback on other marketing opportunities and teach the staff to be ambassadors wherever they go. For example, be sure you and all your staff can comfortably and honestly say that you, too, use Google on a daily basis and why; and make sure that you all can also explain in simple terms why the library's online catalog and full-text databases are different from Google for most academic applications.

Today it is critical that you be able to take the library to your users—outside the library, both electronically and, where appropriate, physically. A colleague recently arranged to have himself and his reference staff set up outside the college cafeteria with computers to provide library "help" to undergraduate students. It has become a popular and well-used approach, and he and his staff are making library friends. In today's online world, going to a library is a bit of an anachronism for many, and if libraries don't find new ways to connect (visually, electronically, and emotionally) with users, they will be phased out by administrators who think they can purchase a subscription to an online library and close the one on campus.

LIBRARY STAFF ENGAGEMENT BEYOND THE LIBRARY

Bragging about your home library is fun; bragging about the library director is even better. At the Gardiner (Maine) Public Library, where I am a trustee, the current library director is also serving as acting city manager. At the University of Maine at Augusta, the dean of libraries is also the dean of distance learning, and in the past served as a campus dean of one of the smaller (six-hundred-student) satellite campuses. The library dean is also on the campus budget committee and cochairs the campus regional accreditation process. What is the point of spreading oneself so thin that it feels like there isn't time enough to do the work of the library? The point is that in the long run, the campus administrators and the faculty members who teach off campus and at a distance see the library director or dean as a team player, someone who might be listened to at crunch time and someone worthy of support if asked.

In higher education, the pecking order is easy to identify: faculty come first, then everyone else. Building a stronger empathetic and collaborative working relationship with faculty members is essential if you hope to generate allies in the budget planning process. A Friends of the Library group made up of influential faculty members and/or area business leaders who understand and believe in what the library is doing can be engaged at budget planning time to testify on behalf of the library or speak privately to decision makers.

It might be time for a disclaimer here: these ideas are designed to level the playing field with the power brokers, not to win greater funds away from other departments at the expense of those departments. What often exists is what I would call a contextual inequity, where those with the power to make decisions or influence others lead intuitively away from supporting the library or library issues because they have an inadequate context (knowledge, awareness, and intuitive sense) from which to judge the library. The context that does exist for many may be from old experiences, previous encounters with the library staff, or something heard from external consultants or so-called experts. Engaging one's self and staff well beyond the library into the arena where university decisions are made will help influence the process of leveling the playing field for the library. If the library director loses an argument on its merit or agrees to a fair share of cutbacks, then he or she has done a good job. If the argument is lost because those in a position of power have a bad impression of the library, its staff, its collections, or the way it is run, then that is indeed the library director's fault.

Bottom line: As the director, it is your responsibility to run a good organization, providing the best resources and services possible with the funds available. It is also your responsibility to develop a strong, positive working relationship with the decision makers above you. In multilibrary organizations, the librarian at the branch campus may need to create linkages with the faculty teaching there and with the campus administrator. For the director, it means finding inroads with the vice president's staff and with the deans, volunteering for committee work, and hosting meetings in the library. Be visible, and be engaged.

STRENGTH IN NUMBERS AND EXTERNAL SUPPORT

As alluded to earlier, building alliances is a useful strategy to offset the negatives of being on the wrong side of campus politics. Some library managers expect the decision-making process to be rational and fair and to always take into account the best arguments; and unfortunately, some others barely show up. Those of us who have been in the business for thirty-plus years likely know of many situations where the squeaky wheel or the most visible department, manager, or apparent friend got the best deal.

Without suggesting that you become cynical about the process, it is important to be forewarned and appropriately prepared. Helping your library prepare for budget activities or the next special project takes an entire community. That's an overused phrase but an important reminder for all of us.

Begin by recognizing that a well-managed, dedicated, and engaged group of supporters (external to the library) is the best ammunition any library director can have at his or her disposal. Engaging them and keeping them interested with real work while you wait for the crisis is not an easy task, however. This, like the task of advertising and marketing the library and serving on important university and campus committees, is among the director's most important work. How to do this and all the library work too is a good question. The answer is that once policies and procedures are fine tuned and staff are trained, the day-to-day operations of the library should essentially run themselves—this should be your goal as a director. Hiring and supporting well-trained staff to provide basic services is the key to leaving yourself room to do what it takes to build alliances and insert yourself into the decision-making fabric of the community.

Make sure your strategic plan has room for an external advisory board or other support organization, and make sure that you have important work for them to do. Not only is an external perspective valuable for assessment purposes (and accountability), but it is the director's very own cheering section. And when cheering isn't enough, board members can twist arms, raise funds, and organize others to support the library.

It is the director's job to make sure the library's external support organization is not placed in an adversarial position with the university decision makers. Little gets accomplished asking for the moon or making arguments that don't match the reality of the budget or the community. If incremental steps are what it takes to get there, then build your long-range plan to accommodate these steps. Advisory or support groups will ideally include some decision makers in the community or university and/or people from well-respected groups and organizations able to support growth and development for the area.

ADVOCACY AND EDUCATION 101

Developing a cohort of supporters, whether a Friends of the Library group in the community or a core group of senior tenured faculty, does not happen overnight. In any community or organization there are those with a proclivity toward libraries. Gather up these people first, make sure they are welcomed and that you have things for them to do, and then invite them to recruit like-minded individuals. Give them visible and important work. Sure, you probably need volunteer help at the front desk from time to time, but even better is work and activities that will connect the Friends and the library with the community. Going to university senate meetings or campus budget and/or planning meetings where the library will be discussed will provide more value. Encourage them to take the library's message outside the library to the arena of the decision makers. Going office to office asking for money in a library fund-raising campaign isn't very practical on a college campus. What has proven easier in one small Maine public library—and might even work on campus—is going office door to office door asking for donations for the library's "annual" auction to raise money for a cause community members can relate to—perhaps a new literature collection, a scholarship fund, or something similar. The auction could be held around a hosted reception or other fun event that would bring people into the library, raise visibility, and plant strong positive feelings about the library and its commitment to the university or college. Alternatively, faculty members could be asked to donate a book from their office collection to be placed in the annual book sale (you need to have one of these) that brings many campus and community members to the library.

In this scenario, you have created a worthwhile project for your volunteers, hopefully identified leaders of the project from within the group, and gotten them out into campus talking to people. Do make sure your team of volunteers contacts nonusers of the library—at least one new contact in each academic department—as well as those who frequent the library, as every contact is a friend-building opportunity. You have also asked potential donors to do something most of them can relate to—donating a favorite book, piece of art or craft, or personal creation for a good cause—the new literature collection for the library. You get the idea.

The library auction and reception can work on the college campus, but other possibilities exist as well—be creative. Gather a core team of faculty and staff (faculty have more clout in the academic world, but staff are needed as well), and visit each faculty member's office with a brochure about the new databases or services for faculty from the library. A brief visit or even a note left with the brochure can have an impact—who else is marketing their internal services to the faculty?

Before you respond by saying you can't raise enough money doing this to make it worthwhile, remember that the goal isn't to make money at all—it's about marketing, promotion, and making friends, all to accomplish the long-term goal of not being left behind at the time of critical budget and strategy sessions as the college plans for the future. Connecting effectively with the community is the only way to build a constituency that can and will support the library both at critical times and every week of the year as library friends work their magic on faculty, deans, and provosts.

Greasing the squeaky wheel is a pretty negative way of thinking about this process, so instead, consider that you are *telling your good story about the library in the most effective way possible—so the decision makers place the library in a position of stature and importance when they have to make critical decisions.*

Do not consider your marketing plan effective until the provost says, "You are too strong an advocate for the library." This actually happened to me, with the then provost comparing my work as library director at budget meetings with that of the other deans, and lamenting that they were not making their cases for increased funding as well.

Bottom line: Getting the daily work of the library done well is a small portion of the work a library director must do. Basic work includes

- long-term planning with a vital strategic plan that includes measurable outcomes and benchmarks—and taking the time to actually measure and report results; and learn from them;
- creating and maintaining a realistic budget; and
- hiring, training, and supporting personnel to become strong managers of their departments.

The other, often overlooked responsibility is that of developing widespread support for the library throughout the community or campus. The director needs a whiteboard in the office with the following:

- Marketing, promotion, and friend-building ideas
- The names of people targeted for support and why
- The person(s) in charge
- The timeline
- The expected outcomes—who can be influenced to help the library long-term

Once a week for ten minutes, in person or on a conference call, the director should provide an update for the core team of contributors, measuring progress and giving out the next assignments. At the end of the month, the director should send a brief report on friend-building out to the entire staff and Friends of the Library group, rewarding and applauding them for their work and successes.

AT THE END OF THE DAY

OK, some of this is a bit extreme, and there aren't a lot of practical ideas about how to avoid the dilemma of having the library treated poorly in funding decisions, or otherwise compromised. Many of us have lived through a number of tough leadership situations, years when most of the collection budget was cut to help stave off a major state revenue shortfall, or situations in which our decisions as library managers were reversed or questioned with prejudice. Things do seem to run in cycles, and eventually leaders with strange ideas go on to other places, budgets are improved, and even state revenues improve. The one constant throughout these experiences, however, is that the library remained open and was well respected as an institution. Fortunately for those of us who work in libraries, libraries are important to the community, even to people who aren't active users; they all seem to see libraries as something that humankind must have access to. Librarians are in the same category, well revered by most—not paid terribly well, but generally revered.

This chapter is about building on the values and impressions that students, faculty members, and children generally share about libraries. The director's job is to find the linkages between these community values about libraries and budgetary and planning decisions. Competition is the ever-present challenge as the library's position among the competing needs of hiring more faculty members, meeting healthcare and insurance costs, and dealing with oil and electricity cost increases. The director's goal is to be sure that the competing departments in the university don't automatically get the biggest share of the budget without libraries' getting a fair hearing. That is all we can ask.

2

Communication

A Two-Way Street

Anne Marie Casey

Communication is a vast, multifaceted topic. The subject of managerial communication in libraries could easily fill a book. In order to keep this chapter to a reasonable length, I primarily treat the communication mistakes of a library middle manger and focus on how to prevent problems in communicating with subordinates.

SEE JANE FAIL TO COMMUNICATE

Jane Handy is the head of the reference department at Western Gulf University (WGU), where she supervises eight reference/instruction librarians. In the last ten years, WGU has reached a level of prominence in the state with distance learning programs. Students can take courses online or at off-campus centers and never have to come to the main campus.

At a recent meeting of library department heads, the director charged the department heads to develop and implement plans to deliver library materials, provide technology support, and offer reference and instruction to students taking online courses or attending class at off-site locations. Currently students must come to the library for most library materials, instruction, or in-depth reference assistance.

Leaving the meeting, Jane was concerned about how well this new charge would come across in the reference department. Chronically short-staffed and constantly faced with new technologies to learn and new programs to support, the reference librarians were already stretched. Having to find a way to provide more instruction and reference services to off-site classes or as part of online classes might be an insurmountable challenge. In addition,

Jane knew there would be opposition among the librarians to this idea. At least one of them, George Young, had voiced the opinion on several occasions that students need to come into the library for instruction and in-depth reference consultations.

Jane decided that the best way to handle the introduction of the distance learning charge was to spring it on the reference department at the next meeting. If George got wind of this new responsibility, he would gather information and rally others in the department to reject the idea. If Jane could get to speak first, she hoped she could head off a lot of fruitless discussion on the subject.

At the end of the next reference meeting, Jane announced to the department that she had a last-minute agenda item. She reported that library administration had directed them to implement additional reference and instruction services for the distance learning students. She knew how hard it would be, but they had to do whatever the administration ordered. After a minute of stunned silence, George loudly demanded to know why the director was ordering a service expansion when everyone knew how overextended the reference librarians were. Jane emphasized that this new service was not her idea but something the administration insisted they undertake with no new resources. She didn't know how they would accomplish it, but she knew they would have to. One of the librarians voiced the opinion that this could be a good idea, but George interrupted and loudly disagreed. As Jane looked around the room, she saw that some librarians were looking down and a few were looking like they wanted to say something but didn't. No one else said anything, so Jane decided to end the meeting.

Afterward, the reference librarians discussed the unexpected agenda item. No one was happy about the additional work expected of them, although several thought it was a good idea to expand services to distance learning students. Over the course of the next few days, the library grapevine buzzed. Everyone had an opinion, and any of the librarians who tried to talk to Jane about it were cut off. She did not want to discuss it. In an attempt to stop all the discussion going on, Jane sent an e-mail message to the reference department on Friday night after the library closed to inform the staff that there would be no further discussion. The department would increase services to distance learners whether they wanted to or not!

No one was happy.

Did Jane do anything right?

Jane's reaction has some serious problems. She may be able to communicate well enough to order a pizza, but she did not do very well with supervisory communication, which includes both upward and downward communication between superiors and subordinates.[1] She does not seem to understand that it is part of her job as supervisor to ensure effective communication in the library. A library manager needs to facilitate communication with subordinates and superiors and among the various people in the department, in the library, and among the constituents the library serves. A manager needs to listen and to share information. "All leaders talk. . . . the leader's most fundamental and important job is to be in touch with those around him or her. Whether it is in the hallways or on the phone, in the middle of the workday or after hours, . . . leaders are involved in a constant series of conversations."[2] Jane seems to operate without that understanding of her role in the library. What did Jane do and how could she have acted differently to avoid the unhappy situation in her department?

VERBAL COMMUNICATION

Jane could have prevented much of the problem right at the beginning by communicating with her colleagues and the library administration in the meeting of department heads. As the representative of the reference department at that meeting, Jane should have asked the director for help in determining how an overextended department could add new services. She should have asked if there was additional funding or staffing available to enable the process. If there was not, then she should have asked what current services could be sacrificed to achieve the new priorities. Having more information from the director on how to carry out this project would have made her communication with the department more productive. The reference librarians would have understood the type of support the administration would give to extending services and realigning priorities as they began their planning discussions.

Another area where Jane missed communicating was with her department head colleagues. At least two other departments received the same charge. Jane could have asked her colleagues to figure out a way for the departments to work together on the new initiative so it would not be as big a burden.

Jane decided to introduce the administrative charge to her department at the staff meeting. That was probably a good idea because it would give them the chance to discuss the issues in one place at one time. However, she dropped the communication ball several times while preparing for and conducting the meeting. She should have shared the agenda item in advance, created an atmosphere that encouraged discussion instead of discouraging it, and allowed time for all points of view to be shared. She did not use the meeting as the opportunity to facilitate the exchange of communication that should have occurred.

The whole idea of a meeting is for a group to communicate, isn't it? Then why do we dread them so much and think that they are a useless waste of time? How many times have most librarians sat through endless meetings where one person controlled the conversation or various people read re-ports? Meetings can sometimes be a series of never-ending discussions on the same topic with nothing accomplished. However, they do not have to be the endless waste of time that many of us think they are. A good man-ager, who learns how to run an effective meeting, can make them what they are meant to be: a forum for the exchange of ideas, the development of new processes, and the accomplishment of tasks in a group. It is the responsibil-ity of the manager to communicate essential points, lead a discussion on the topics, encourage feedback from everyone, and keep the meeting on schedule. Some ways to accomplish these things are to ask for input on the agenda, give the group in advance any information or documents on issues that will be discussed, deliver the facts honestly and objectively, ask for feedback, support discussion, control the conversation so that one voice or opinion doesn't drown out the others, be aware of common nonverbal cues that show a person is nervous or wants to speak up and encourage people exhibiting these cues to share their opinions, work to achieve consensus, and end the meeting on time!

Jane didn't add the potentially controversial agenda item in advance because she didn't want an argument about it before the meeting. She an-nounced it in a very tentative way, voiced her concern for the burden it would place on the department, and stated that it was an administrative directive. Her attitude toward the idea was communicated to the staff in such a way that it was clear she was not happy with the idea. How can the department then see it in a positive light? "No matter how great people think an idea is, they are not likely to pursue it with much enthusiasm if their bosses or others they depend upon for support are indifferent or disapproving. By demonstrating real enthusiasm for the new ideas, leaders can create a safe space to release others' interest in the ideas."[3] If she had said that the department had an exciting new charge to expand services and would find some way to prioritize and streamline to be able to take on this expansion, she might have had a more positive response. The people with strong oppositional views would have still spoken up, but the librarians who were positive or neutral about the idea may have been more willing to speak up too.

Allowing some heated discussion in a meeting is a valid way to ensure communication on controversial topics. "Conflict is absolutely vital to productive interactions. . . . It is only when we disagree about some-thing—when we look from different perspectives or when we make differ-ent interpretations—that there is really anything to talk about."[4] The key point is that controversial subjects need to be discussed in a professional atmosphere where librarians are informed and have the opportunity to express their opinions without being shouted down. Everyone needs the opportunity to ask questions and voice opinions. Jane should have encouraged the librarians who did not approve of the new charge to explain why. She should have encouraged those who saw it as a positive change to speak up as well. Most of us are locked into one way of seeing or doing things, and we gain perspective by hearing other points of view. By listening to what everyone contributes to a discussion, a manager can lead team planning that considers different possibilities and different personalities. Plans developed from consensus are generally better accepted because all points of view are considered.

Anytime a department is faced with the challenge of changing the way it has traditionally operated, there is bound to be some controversy. The more information people have, the better they can deal with change. The charge to add new services was a very important one that needed to be communicated to the reference staff immediately. Jane could have sent an e-mail message to the reference department introducing the subject and asking the librarians to prepare for a special discussion at their next staff meeting. Instead, she shared the news unannounced at the meeting, let one librarian explode, and then cut discussion off without trying to encourage the others to speak up. This was a big deal. The reference librarians needed to talk, so they did, on the grapevine. The reference grapevine was active after the staff meeting because questions had been left unanswered, there was dissension, and nothing had been resolved. Jane was not open to talking about the issue, so the librarians talked among themselves, expressing fears and anger and not being able to resolve anything.

Human beings need to communicate about issues that affect their lives. They need open communication channels. If they don't have them, they will communicate informally trying to find out what they need to know. Informal communication can be very good because it helps staff to talk through issues in a nonthreatening setting, but it can also spread anxiety and perpetuate misinformation. Several studies link good managerial communication to job satisfaction[5] and prove that in a time of change, management needs to be especially aware of keeping communication open.[6] Unfortunately, communication can break down in the workplace during times of change because everyone is busier and because change can breed conflict. Most of us seem to do our best to avoid conflict.

Jane could not have prevented the buzzing on the grapevine after the meeting even if she had led a good discussion at the staff meeting. Individual meetings are an excellent place for a manager to communicate better. In a private meeting, there is more time to ask questions, to listen, to observe nonverbal cues, and to take the time to address issues that are more important or interesting to one person than they are to the entire group. One-on-one meetings with the manager give staff members who need time or have trouble speaking up in a group the opportunity to ask questions and be heard. Such meetings are often the best place for a manager to ask questions in a nonthreatening atmosphere to learn about what staff members need and what their goals are. "Leaders, through questions, can build a culture in which questions are welcomed, assumptions are challenged, and new ways to solve problems are explored."[7] Jane could have used the combination of private, one-on-one meetings with the grapevine to generate clearer, less fear-driven thinking among the reference librarians. Jane knew that George was against providing new services to distance learners, but she didn't know why. If she had asked George to talk about his objections in a private meeting, she would have understood his objections better and been able to either help him get past them or, if he convinced her that his objections were realistic, relay those concerns to her supervisor.

WRITTEN COMMUNICATION

In twenty-first-century libraries, most employees have very busy schedules and can work a variety of schedules. Written communication is a good way to be sure that everyone receives the same information. Jane could have used e-mail at several points to increase communication. She not only missed several good opportunities, but when she finally did use e-mail, she did the worst possible thing: she decreed an end to the discussion. Jane could have e-mailed the director after the department heads' meeting to ask more questions about the new charge. She could have e-mailed information on the charge to the reference staff before the staff meeting. She could have followed the staff meeting with an e-mail discussion. Not everyone communicates effectively in a meeting. Using e-mail to inform before the meeting and to follow up after opens the communication channels for more people to express their opinions and ask questions. The only time she used e-mail was to cut off discussion, and that is the worst possible use of it.

E-mail can be one of the best forms of communication in the workplace. "For the leader, the advantage is being able to contact every member of the group, provide the exact same message to each person, solicit information, and have every member respond—without even one face-to-face or real time contact. Email's strong suit is that people can examine and access data at their own different paces and thoughtfully prepare their individual feedback. Its influence on communication and management has been revolutionary."[8] Every library department should have an electronic list that they use for discussion and information. In my experience, one of the best examples of good, regular departmental communication was in an institution where several librarians worked from isolated one-person offices and used an electronic list to communicate. They "talked" daily on the departmental list, discussing difficult reference questions, sharing information, planning for new developments and services, and having informal personal conversations. They worked together as a far more cohesive team than a similar department in the same library where librarians' offices were side by side but where they rarely communicated as a group except in weekly meetings.

CONCLUSION

"Clear communication that moves toward results may seem easy, but it is not. In fact, communication is rarely clear, consistent and forward moving. Rather, it usually suffers the pitfalls of misunderstood fact and misinterpreted emotion. Furthermore, most communication about difficult issues is characterized by circuitous argument, uncertain outcomes, lack of clarity, conflicts in personality, and misaligned goals."[9]

The five basic types of communication are speaking, listening, writing, reading, and nonverbal communication. Many managers focus far more on speaking and writing than on listening and reading. It is easy for a manager to fall into the habit of thinking of communication as a one-way street, "how I let you know what the administration and I expect from you at work," rather than as a dialogue, "how I understand things from your perspective or how you understand them from mine." Listening is probably the most important communication skill a manager can have, and it is probably the most ignored.

The communication skills necessary for a good manager are more extensive than those needed for normal interpersonal communication. An effective leader learns to adapt communication styles in order to most effectively advance agendas, share learning, and build stronger relationships.[10] The way to do this differs according to the audience and the situation. It is important for a manager to be aware of his or her own communication style and to understand how to adapt when communication is not occurring. To assume that communication occurs every time two people talk to each other would be a mistake. People do not always listen; they are more interested in what they have to say than in how the other person receives and processes it; they imply rather than speak directly; they make incorrect assumptions based on preconceived notions, ethnic background, or education; and they miss nonverbal cues.

Perfect communication is not possible in this life. There are pitfalls everywhere to truly communicating what we think, feel, or want, and to understanding what someone else is trying to tell us. There are so many things that get in the way of communication: assumptions, personality, ethnic and gender differences, not listening, talking too much, misunderstanding. It is hard work to communicate. It is harder work to communicate as a middle manager because an important part of the job is funneling communication between upper management and library workers. The effective library manager, who is aware of his or her role as a facilitator of communication from department to administration and back, asks questions, listens to the answers, encourages staff to ask questions, uses other forms of communication if one form is not working, asks for input and gives feedback, communicates enthusiasm for a new project, controls the conversation in meetings so all contribute and no one dominates, communicates by e-mail, encourages discussion on electronic lists, informs the department and administration regularly, and watches for common nonverbal cues. Most importantly, a library manager who is a good communicator is flexible and willing to try new ways to understand and be understood.

NOTES

1. Phillip G. Clampitt and Cal W. Downs, "Employee Perceptions of the Relationship between Communication and Productivity," *Journal of Business Communication* 30, no. 1 (1993): 6.

2. Phil Harkins, *Powerful Conversations: How High-Impact Leaders Communicate* (New York: McGraw-Hill, 1999), 3.

3. Gail T. Fairhurst and Robert A. Sarr, *The Art of Framing: Managing the Language of Leadership* (San Francisco: Jossey-Bass, 1996), 57.

4. Barbara Conroy and Barbara Schindler Jones, *Improving Communication in the Library* (Phoenix: Oryx Press, 1986), 94.

5. Clampitt and Downs, "Employee Perceptions," 6; John D. Pettit, Jose R. Goris, and Bobby C. Vaught, "An Examination of Organizational Communication as a Moderator of the Relationship between Job Performance and Job Satisfaction," *Journal of Business Communication* 34, no. 1 (1997): 81–98; John J. Trombetta and Donald P. Rogers, "Communication Climate, Job Satisfaction, and Organizational Commitment," *Management Communication Quarterly* 1, no. 4 (1988): 494–514.

6. Mardi Chalmers, Theresa Liedtka, and Carol Bednar, "A Library Communication Audit for the Twenty-First Century," *portal: Libraries and the Academy* 6, no. 2 (2006): 186.

7. Michael Marquardt, *Leading with Questions* (San Francisco: Jossey-Bass, 2005), 27.

8. Scott Snair, *Stop the Meeting I Want to Get Off!* (New York: McGraw-Hill, 2003), 155.

9. Harkins, *Powerful Conversations*, 6.

10. Harkins, *Powerful Conversations*, 166.

3

Effective Project Management

The Key to Success with Information Technology

Frank Cervone

When the libraries of Western Pennsylvania University at Pitcairn (WPU-P) embarked on their project to bring a "next-generation" library catalog to campus, everyone was excited. The staff at WPU-P felt that the introduction of leading-edge technology would both provide faculty and students with greater access to library resources as well as establish the library as a leader in technology innovation.

In the negotiations before the contract was signed, the vendor assured the project team that customization of the user interface could be accomplished in less than a day with its exclusive "point-and-click" customization application. Furthermore, loading of MARC data would be a simple matter of nightly batch data transfers. Although this would mean that there would be a delay in getting new material into the enhanced interface, no one on the project team felt this would be a problem.

However, not too long after the initial installation of the software, some problems began to develop. Based on the assurance from the vendor that the user interface could be modified through the point-and-click customization application, the project team had only estimated one day of work for the user interface customization. When the reference staff complained that simply adding the library's logo and changing the background colors to conform to university standards would not suffice, the project timeline started to extend. As discussions continued, the project team was informed that additional functionalities in the form of uniform title and genre searches were "absolutely necessary" for a day-one production rollout.

Undaunted, the project team investigated the issues related to creating both uniform title and genre indexes. As they continued to work with the issue, it became clear that the project team did not have the resources to do

19

the programming necessary to create the two indexes, so consultants were brought in to develop them.

When the original deadline for a functioning test system came and went, the library director was concerned, but did not say anything to the project team leader in the belief that the problems were just due to minor delays and that soon everything would be back on track.

Days turned to weeks, and still there was no functioning test system. Much of the delay was blamed on the significant delays in creating the genre index. The project team explained to the director that the consultants had to write numerous programs to perform data cleanup on all the MARC records already in the catalog. While this work was going on, most of the project team was left idle.

Eventually though, the work on the records was complete and the first run of the data load was attempted. Although it did complete successfully, the load took three times longer than had been initially estimated. At that rate, it would be just barely possible to load all the records from the library management system into the new catalog every night.

After four months of delays, the new system was ready to go, and the library unveiled the new interface, now known as "NGSearch" for next-generation search, with great fanfare. Advertisements were taken out in the student newspaper, and faculty members were sent personalized notices about the new interface. Everyone in the library felt quite confident in the work that had been accomplished. So, it was with great surprise that the director opened the student newspaper the following week and found a long editorial entitled "NGSearch—As in No Good." With rising anxiety, the director read a litany of student complaints on how slow the system was, how confusing it was, and how it did not meet their needs for an advanced research tool as it only provided information about traditional library materials.

In hastily put together focus groups with students, the project team learned that adding the uniform title search caused all other title searches to slow down significantly whenever the search involved a record with a uniform title. Additionally, the uniform title and genre searches confused students as they did not understand the purpose of these searches. Finally, the students complained that what they really needed was a system that searched *all* the resources of the library, both traditional and electronic, in one fell swoop.

Eventually, WPU-P worked out the problems, but at great expense. In addition to the loss of credibility with students, the library sustained significant cost overruns in implementation, cost overruns that had to be absorbed by the materials budget in the following fiscal year.

All these problems could be traced back to grievous errors in project management.

THE CHALLENGE OF INFORMATION TECHNOLOGY PROJECT MANAGEMENT

Few would question that managing information technology projects is a challenge. Often, when projects roll out on time and on budget, people are surprised. In fact, it has almost become acceptable practice for projects to incur overruns as an inevitable outcome of uncertainty within the project implementation environment. Nevertheless, this perspective is flawed because well-managed projects are possible even in the most dynamic and unpredictable environments. What is required is a solid understanding of project management and a firm commitment of management to adhere to these best practices.

There are many reasons why projects fail. In this chapter, we'll explore issues related to project failure in the information technology area and consider some of the possible responses to situations where failure is likely.

However, before beginning, we must have a solid understanding of what a project actually is. It is important to distinguish between projects and operational activities because the management of these two types of activities differs, sometimes significantly depending on the local environment. Thus, we should not expect to manage a project the same way we manage day-to-day activities within the library.

A succinct description of a project is a temporary sequence of unique, complex, and connected activities having one goal or purpose that must be completed by a specific time, within a defined budget, and according to specification.[1] Based on this definition, we can make a distinction between projects, which have a definite end to the sequences of their activities, and operational tasks, which tend to be repeated in a cyclic manner with no distinct endpoint. For example, an upgrade to a new version of a library management system would clearly be a project, rather than an operational activity, as it has a definite end point: the final cutover to the new version of the system. Cataloging and circulating material, however, are operational activities because they are done routinely and we do not expect them to end at a specific time.

This last distinction is somewhat obscure as there may well be repeating elements in a project, such as programming. However, if the overall sequence and nature of the activities result in a unique outcome that has a distinct termination point, the sequence of activities qualifies as a project.

HOW PROJECTS ARE UNDERMINED

There are, as a rule, many signs that a project may be in trouble, but one of the most difficult to overcome, yet frequently overlooked, indicators is an

environment that is hostile to the project. Hostile environments are particularly dangerous because in reaction to anxiety related to change, the right set
of circumstances and opportunities can lead people to sabotage a project.[2]
All too often, naive project managers fail to understand the political context
in which they are operating and the subsequent consequences the environment can have on the outcome of a project. A clear indicator of a political
problem is when the project manager cannot get important stakeholders
to participate in activities related to the feasibility study. Unquestionably,
behavior of this nature is a clear indicator of a hostile environment.

Therefore, during the initial stages of a project, and especially during the
feasibility study, the major political issues and obstacles related to the project must be resolved. Approaching the problem in steps, by first uncovering
and then addressing the objections of various constituencies, is the most
effective way of defusing political problems. Ignoring them will not make
them go away. It is also important that the project manager tackle these
problems early on in the project life cycle. This cannot be left to later stages
of the project as by then it may be too late; failing to address the issues early
risks undermining the subsequent phases of the project.

Another significant factor in project success is how an organization deals
with risky propositions. In an environment where failure is not tolerated
well, projects are especially vulnerable to failure due to technical, economic,
or organizational reasons. When the negative consequences of taking a risk
overshadow the benefits of a successful outcome, the innovative behaviors
associated with most project implementations are unlikely to occur as the
primary concern of staff will be on minimizing risk.[3] As managers, we must
avoid creating environments where it is "disloyal" to talk about the down-
side of a project plan.[4] One way of avoiding this is to create an environment where honest, open, and transparent communication is encouraged
throughout the organization. In such an environment, we are better able
to ensure that the balance of risk and reward is worthwhile to the involved
staff, as being involved in activities that have high risks usually requires a
high reward at the outcome.[5]

The last major factor in how projects are undermined is when objectives
are not clearly defined. A project in this state is often typified by an environment where the requirements are essentially unmanaged[6] and as a consequence vacillate, change, and are modified with no apparent justification
as the project moves forward. A common cause of this problem is project
sponsors who lack the experience or vocabulary to describe requirements in
adequate detail, which results in vague or ambiguous objectives.

More often, however, the vague objectives are due to the project team's
not understanding all the project issues.[7] Defining crisp, unambiguous
requirements for a project takes time, energy, and extensive communication with people from throughout the organization and (usually) external

constituency groups. That is, project managers must talk to all levels of staff and patrons who will use a proposed new system. Obtaining requirements only from a single user group, be that library managers or staff members in a particular functional area within the library, will inevitably lead to a project fraught with problems.

While this type of broad communication inherently involves more time, it is time well spent. Management can present an idealized version of "what works," and staff in particular functional areas can present idealized versions of "what should be," but these may be quite different from or completely at odds with the day-to-day reality our constituencies need or expect. Therefore, it cannot be emphasized enough that all concerned parties must be involved in defining requirements, no matter how simple a project may appear to be.

ADDRESSING ISSUES THAT CAN UNDERMINE A PROJECT

Good planning is the key to any project's success. In the typical information technology project, activities can be grouped into one of five categories: project initiation and feasibility analysis; design; execution and production; monitoring and controlling; and review and termination.[8] When planning in any of these phases is skipped or circumvented, the foundational work of the entire project is compromised.

Unfortunately, people often see detailed planning as a waste of time. In general, there are two major factors that contribute to this mindset. To some degree, unfavorable attitudes toward project planning are the result of cynicism. If all that results in the end is a series of charts and reports that are never referred to in a meaningful way, people distrust the process. On the other hand, some may see the plan as a straitjacket that constrains the creativity of project members, ultimately resulting in an inflexible project outline that prevents necessary activities from being performed. In system development teams, it is not uncommon to find project team members who are simply impatient with the planning process. These folks just want to jump right in and start working as they feel time is better spent doing "real work" rather than engaging in planning.

In the end, though, none of these are acceptable reasons for bypassing or short-circuiting the planning process. Planning is crucial for a number of reasons, but perhaps most importantly it presents the best opportunity for the project manager to generate "buy-in" and resolve conflicts regarding project requirements.[9]

In a well-managed planning process, all the appropriate people will have a chance to contribute to the plan in meaningful ways with a minimum amount of overhead. When done correctly, planning results in a project plan that contains detailed information related to what needs to be done, by whom, and when. Repeated success with a well-managed planning process provides a way for an organization to demonstrate the value of planning.[10] Moreover, by combining traditional project management with agile methods,[11] a project manager can alleviate the concerns that a rigorous planning process will become a constraint on the project overall.[12]

On the other hand, agility needs to be tempered by appropriate management of expectations. As a project develops, it is not uncommon for the project manager to be asked to add additional functionality or features. While in many cases, these additional requests are worthwhile, the project manager must balance this worthiness with the need to complete the project within a reasonable time frame and budget. Managers who do not manage this are typically faced with the classic problems of scope creep and feature creep.

Scope creep occurs when unexpected and (usually) uncontrolled growth of user expectations and requirements occurs as a project progresses. An example of extreme scope creep would be when the redesign of a portion of a website blossoms into the implementation of a content management system. Feature creep differs from scope creep in that it is the uncontrolled addition of features or functionality to a system in development, most often without regard to how this will affect either project cost or scheduling. This commonly occurs when a system analyst or programmer adds functionality not requested during the requirements definition. This anticipation of future functionality requests is usually performed with good intentions, typically to add value to the product. Nevertheless, it is a problem for three reasons. First, the additional functionality may not be desired. Second, for various reasons the additional functionality may have been intentionally deferred to some time in the future. Third, the additional features will inevitably add to the project timeline and budget, resulting in overruns in both areas.[13]

Addressing scope and feature creep should begin during the requirements phase. Once all the project requirements have been gathered, all project participants should review them. This review is an excellent opportunity for the project manager to educate the involved parties about the problems related to scope and feature creep. By providing this information about the dangers of creep, the project manager is in a better position to obtain agreement from everyone that they will work to avoid creating situations that could lead to either type of creep.

Scope and feature creep can be confounding factors in the problem that arises due to incorrect estimation of the effort that must go into a project. In order to deliver a successful project, the project manager must use some methodology for getting reasonable estimates of the cost and effort in performing various project-related activities.[14] Simply guessing what will be required does not work because when guesswork is used, the likelihood of significantly underestimating is just as great as the likelihood of overestimating. This occurs because effort is often assumed to be equal to duration. Effort within a task is the amount of time it will take to complete a task based on an idealized schedule. This is based on the assumption that there will be no interruptions, breaks, or wasted time. Duration, in contrast, is the time the task will take to complete when all overhead and waiting time (which includes work breaks, meetings, travel time, and all other time not devoted to direct work on the project) is taken into account.

Accurate estimates are created by decomposing the project into specific deliverables via a work breakdown structure (WBS), a hierarchical arrangement of all the pieces of work within the project.[15] While the WBS does not inherently reflect dependencies among the various project tasks, it typically does reflect interrelationships among deliverables of the project. One of the main reasons for creating the WBS is to prevent creating a project plan that is too vague or general as a result of specifying tasks that have ill-defined deliverables. This is guarded against by breaking down the project deliverables into very specific detail.

With a completed WBS in hand, a project manager can accurately determine the start-to-finish relationships between various activities in the project, known as the project dependencies, as a prelude to creating an overall project timeline. Depending on the nature of the project, many activities can be carried out simultaneously; however, it is far more likely that most project activities can only start once another activity is completed and approved. Charting the dependencies between various activities is critical as it helps us understand the multiple pathways through the tasks in a project, which in turn inform us of how delays in one area can affect the overall project timeline.

The most important path a manager must monitor is the *critical path*, the sequence of activities that will take the longest time to complete in the project.[16] Any deviation from schedule in the critical path will extend the duration of the entire project.

Work breakdown structures are also useful devices for inhibiting premature commitment to project specifics. In every project, the project manager must have enough time to perform a proper evaluation of the time and resources required to do the project. Projects that are put into place with a predetermined start and end date, before adequate analysis has been performed, are doomed to fail. Until the project team members have been assigned to specific activities and the duration of each activity in the project has been projected, it is impossible to know how long the project will really take to complete.

Premature commitment can potentially cascade into a different type of problem. It is not uncommon for a project to fall behind schedule when an unrealistic timeline has been established, but even in the best of circumstances, a project can fall behind. The most common response to this dilemma is to add more personnel to the project. This, however, is an inherently ineffective technique as it actually slows the project down even further.[17] Assuming that there was a reasonable schedule in the first place, the only way schedule slippage can be avoided is by proactively paying close attention to deviations in the project timeline. As soon as schedule slippage is identified, the project manager should attempt to alleviate the problem with existing staff. If that is not possible and new staff must be added to the project, the project manager must ensure the new members are not trained by staff working on critical path activities. Diverting any staff on the critical path from their tasks will just further exacerbate delays in the project.

THE BLURRY BOUNDARY WHERE PEOPLE AND PROCESS MANAGEMENT SKILLS MEET

Most library information technology projects require a diverse range of skills, but unfortunately, many teams lack the breadth and depth they require to accomplish everything in the project. In most organizations, this is simply because the size of our staff prevents us from having all the required expertise in house. Even in large organizations, it is rare to have expert staff available in every project area. Addressing this involves several strategies.

If we are not sure a staffing shortcoming exists, the senior technical staff should interview the applicable project staff to make certain they have the necessary skill sets for the tasks to which they will be assigned. If, as a result of this review, it appears that staffing constraints will cause a key component within a project to be inadequately addressed in house, the project manager must either build additional training into the project budget or allocate funds to bring in outside help. Simply trying to limp along without adequate staffing will not result in a successful project outcome.

Related to this problem is the common mistake where a project manager assigns an employee who is good in one area to a related, yet distinct, area and expects the employee to be just as exemplary in this new area. For example, it may well be that without additional training, an outstanding monographic cataloger may be adrift if charged with the creation of a detailed taxonomy of the library's website.

Savvy project managers must also be attentive to the development of camaraderie within the project team. The four classic stages in the formation of a team are forming, storming, norming, and performing.[18] A team must be given time to go through all the stages if the organization expects to receive quality work from the team members. When the team is in the forming stage, they are becoming familiar with the project and determining both who the other people in the project are and how they relate to each other and the project overall. In smaller organizations, this stage may not need to occur in every project, but it will be a necessary stage in larger organizations for almost all projects.

Once the forming stage is complete, the group enters the storming stage, where ideas are developed and relationships are worked out. Intense debate can occur during this stage; this is normal and should be expected. After these issues have been worked out, the team enters the norming phase as they come to general agreement on acceptable behaviors, practices, and values. Only after all this has occurred does the project really get moving.

The project manager needs to be closely attuned to developments in these stages. During these stages, a major role of the project manager is to act as facilitator as well as manager of the group. To be truly effective, the manager must carefully consider his or her own preferences in management and interaction with others and work to reach out in alternative ways to others who have different preferences in being managed and different styles of interaction.

WHAT MAKES FOR SUCCESS, THEN?

Having effective project managers is one of the critical links in organizational success with project-based work. People who provide effective motivation or encouragement of others, encourage ideas and contributions from others, deal with conflict effectively, and are able to "take the heat" when unpopular decisions need to be made are the most effective project managers.

Managing expectations is a critical skill as the project manager is always striving to achieve a balance between enabling change and constraining unbridled deviation from the project goals. Unconstrained deviation from project goals occurs when too many changes are applied to a project, which results in a different project emerging at the end of the process than was planned for at the beginning. Therefore, the best project managers are adept at balancing the need to maintain stability of initial goals throughout a project against the folly of adhering to initial requirements that have been transformed in the face of dramatic change.

Formal research into project management indicates that a wide variety of factors are integral to project success. When the Standish Group[19] interviewed IT managers and asked what were the most important aspects in making a project successful, an interesting aspect that arose from the research is that there is no single factor that ensures project success. The top factor, user involvement, was cited by only 15.9 percent of the respondents. If one were to create a list of the most significant factors in project success, many factors could come into play. However, reviews of the project management literature repeatedly and consistently point to some critical aspects:

- Clearly define objectives at the project outset and do not jump to a solution before the problem is fully understood.
- Provide the opportunity for all concerned constituencies to give input and guidance in relation to project objectives and outcomes on an ongoing basis throughout the life of the project.
- Carefully assess the ability to manage and perform the project with the available resources and obtain additional resources if necessary.
- Ensure that support by upper management is in place as well as support by the managers in the areas that will be affected by the project.

Subsequent studies have indicated that one of the most critical factors in a successful project implementation is not technical functionality, but rather cultural acceptance.[20] Information technology projects frequently force fundamental change in the way individuals and groups interact and function. Subsequent cultural shifts may occur within the organization, but we cannot underestimate the time, education, training, and staff buy-in those shifts may require. Consequently, without a major investment in developing a culture that accepts and adapts to change, it is very difficult to implement a project that is fundamentally new and different from the status quo; therefore, without a fundamental cultural change, we cannot expect to implement anything except for the most superficial, incremental change.[21]

Good project managers are talented and multifaceted people who, most importantly, know how to form effective teams. One senior project manager I know has described his job as "removing obstacles" from the path of the project team to make it more possible for the team to accomplish its work. Clearly, the work of a project manager is not simply that of a technologist. A project manager must be able to pull disparate elements together, seemingly from nothing, to create something outstanding.

People who provide effective motivation or encouragement for others, encourage ideas and contributions from others, deal with conflict effectively, and are able to "'take the heat" when unpopular decisions need to be made can be effective as project managers. All these qualities are critical to the effectiveness of a project manager and to the success of an organization's projects.

NOTES

1. Robert K. Wysocki, Robert Beck, and David B. Crane, *Effective Project Management*, 2nd ed. (New York: Wiley, 2002).

2. John Murray, "Uncovering Hidden Agendas," *IT Manager's Journal*, January 16, 2006, http://www.itmanagersjournal.com/articles/10253 (accessed March 12, 2007).

3. A. M. Alquier and M. H. Tignol, "Project Management Technique to Estimate and Manage Risk of Innovative Projects" (paper presented at International Project Management Association symposium, Stockholm, Sweden, May 31–June 1, 2001).

4. Heather A. Smith, James D. McKeen, and D. Sandy Staples, "Risk Management in Information Systems: Problems and Potential," *Communications of the Association for Information Systems* 7, no. 13 (2001): 1–27.

5. David L. Hamil, "Your Mission, Should You Choose to Accept It: Project Management Excellence," GeoCommunity, 2005, http://spatialnews.geocomm.com/features/mesa1 (accessed March 7, 2007).

6. R. J. Torres, *Practitioner's Handbook for User Interface Design and Development*, Software Quality Institute Series (Upper Saddle River, N.J.: Prentice-Hall, 2001).

7. Dov Dvir, Tzvi Raz, and Aaron J. Shenhar, "An Empirical Analysis of the Relationship between Project Planning and Project Success," *International Journal of Project Management* 21, no. 2003 (2003): 89–95.

8. Wysocki, Beck, and Crane, *Effective Project Management.*

9. John M. Bryson, Philip Bromiley, and Yoon Soo Jung, "Influences of Context and Process on Project Planning Success," *Journal of Planning Education and Research* 9, no. 3 (1990): 183–95.

10. Harold Kerzner, *Strategic Planning for Project Management Using a Project Management Maturity Model* (New York: Wiley, 2001), 91.

11. Doug DeCarlo, "Get It Right the Last Time: Developing an Agile Attitude," *gantthead.com*, September 5, 2006, http://www.gantthead.com/article.cfm?ID=232803 (accessed March 21, 2007).

12. Barry Boehm, "Get Ready for Agile Methods, with Care," *Computer* 35, no. 1 (2002): 64–69.

13. Brenda Whitaker, "What Went Wrong? Unsuccessful Information Technology Projects," *Information Management & Computer Security* 7, no. 1 (1999): 23–30.

14. Steve McConnell, *Rapid Development: Taming Wild Software Schedules* (Redmond, Wash.: Microsoft Press, 1996).

15. R. C. Tausworthe, "The Work Breakdown Structure in Software Project Management," *Journal of Systems and Software* 1 (1980): 181–86.

16. H. M. Soroush, "The Most Critical Path in a Pert Network," *Journal of the Operational Research Society* 45, no. 3 (1994): 287–300.

17. Frederick P. Brooks, *The Mythical Man-Month: Essays on Software Engineering* (Reading, Mass.: Addison-Wesley Professional, 1995).

18. K. Mackey, "Stages of Team Development," *Software* 16, no. 4 (1999): 90–91.

19. Standish Group, "The Chaos Report (1994)," 1994, http://www.standishgroup.com/sample_research/chaos_1994_1.php (accessed March 10, 2007); Standish Group, "Unfinished Voyages: A Follow-up to the Chaos Report," 1995, http://www.standishgroup.com/sample_research/unfinished_voyages_1.php (accessed March 10, 2007).

20. Alexander Laufer and Edward J. Hoffman, *Project Management Success Stories: Lessons of Project Leaders* (New York: Wiley, 2000); Terry Cooke-Davies, "The "Real"

Success Factors on Projects," *International Journal of Project Management* 20, no. 2002 (2002): 185–90; M. Sumner, "Critical Success Factors in Enterprise Wide Information Management Systems Projects" (paper presented at ACM SIGCPR Conference on Computer Personnel Research, New Orleans, La., April 8–10, 1999).

21. Quy Nguyen Huy, "Emotional Capability, Emotional Intelligence, and Radical Change," *The Academy of Management Review* 24, no. 2 (1999): 325–45.

4

Staffing for Success

Connie Costantino

While reflecting on how to avoid mistakes with staffing in library management, I realized that the errors made usually surface from problems within three critical areas. Their order of importance is relevant, too:

1. People
2. Strategies
3. Change

Yes, people are at the top! They are the most important and most complicated element of management, so there are an infinite number of mistakes to avoid. Many theories contribute to methods of successful staffing in the field of management. Within the realm of academic libraries, David A. Baldwin and Robert L. Migneault offer a solid foundation for managers. Their theory is rooted in a humanistic approach that utilizes teamwork.[1] Camila A. Alire wraps Baldwin and Migneault's theory into a neat package by adding that "common sense management still drives the way many administrators work with their staff no matter which organizational theory is in place. When common sense is coupled with a humanistic approach to management, the result is a practice that could affect most management theories."[2]

Three scenarios follow. Each contains opposite approaches to managing library staffing and will present mistakes along with solutions (humanistic and common-sense) to avoid them. Change management strategies include implementing staff development, training, and evaluation. I hope you can use these processes as tools to help you avoid similar or even different mistakes.

ERROR 1: PEOPLE

Mistake

Mary Lou, a library manager, starts a new job and doesn't take time to get to know the staff or what they are doing. She also doesn't let the staff get to know her. This lack of communication with no sense of direction results in low staff morale, unfriendly library services, and information resources that are not used. The staff and users at Unhappy Library are frustrated.

Solution

Anthony, a new library manager, starts his job by doing the following:

1. He makes staff top priority. Anthony not only introduces himself to each library staff member, but he also makes appointments to meet one-on-one with each person. During these sessions, Anthony asks many questions regarding the person's tasks and responsibilities. He speaks audibly and clearly with emphasis on key issues to be sure he is understood. He explains he wants to know what is working well and what improvements will benefit the staff. He thinks before he speaks and considers how his questions may impact others. Anthony realizes that respect is a foundation of good relationships. He maintains an open-door policy except when he is in a meeting or on a deadline. In these cases, a red flag is displayed outside his door. He encourages other staff members to use this communication tool too.

2. He listens carefully. Anthony is amazed at the quantity of useful answers he hears regarding the who, what, where, when, why, and how of each staff member's situation. He takes careful notes, explaining that he wants to remember these facts and useful information so that the Happy Library team can create a plan to make their jobs better and more productive. Anthony also asks them what questions they have. He continues to take notes so that he can follow up with answers after perusing the questions.

3. He leads by example. Anthony is a born leader because he practices what he preaches. In the world of business, he "walks the talk." When he says "Good morning" to everyone he sees (no matter what their position level), the staff realize that he is sincere. Anthony walks into the room looking neat and professional, dressed well but conservatively, and expects his staff to follow suit. Staff members find themselves pleasantly surprised because Anthony often says "nice job" for small tasks. The staff are impressed that he notices these details and expresses his appreciation. Then there's Anthony's constant "thank

you"—just two words that mean a whole dictionary! In addition to all this, Anthony is always positive, reliable, consistent, and ethical; never assumes anything; and takes pride in every member of the Happy Library team's performance. Oh yes, if Anthony sees a book out of order or scrap paper on the floor . . . you guessed it!

4. He develops patience and envisions, not a glass half full, but a whole new glass! As a new library manager, Anthony reflects on his first month and is surprised at the amount of time, effort, genuine concern, and interest he has invested in each member of the library staff, but he also realizes that this quality time with each person is an opportunity not only to get to know each other but also to motivate and encourage them to do their best . . . to reach for the stars! In the information age, it's been called "thinking outside the box." Anthony paraphrases a managerial slogan he read one day in a leadership brochure: "It used to be that the glass was half-empty or half-full. Now you have to re-engineer the glass."

The staff begins to develop new ways to do things to enhance their environment. They subscribe to the Google newsletter for librarians[3] and surprise themselves by learning ways they can enhance their service with help from what used to be their "competitor"—they never dreamed that Google could be a partner! Of course, it helps that Anthony continually admits his own mistakes, which demonstrates that everyone at Happy Library is human! It is obvious that Anthony is passionate about his beliefs in the benefits and value of an efficient and effective library system. His staff quickly become his "raving fans" and not just "satisfied" staff.[4]

In reflecting on his team's excellent performance in solving library users' problems, Anthony was elated that the time he spent in adjusting to each staff member's needs and personality was time well spent. The attitudinal change in the staff's mindset made him realize the benefits of the strategies he used to direct and guide the Happy Library team.

ERROR 2: STRATEGIES

Mistake

Betty, a library manager for a few years, dealt with each day as it came and wondered why her library had the reputation of being called the High-Turnover-in-Staff Library. Staff members didn't know to whom they reported, and they also didn't know what they were supposed to do. This confusion carried over to the people who came into the library because library users were given different answers depending on whom they asked.

Not many people used the library, but those who did usually left without the information they needed.

Solution

Bertha, an experienced library manager, was called in to save the day. She had taken a strategic management planning course from Dr. H. Igor Ansoff[5] as an interdisciplinary option during her master's in library and information science program. Dr. Ansoff taught her that the functions that were common in managing a successful business were the same processes used to manage life. Bertha realized these functions transferred into her library career path.

So after implementing Anthony's Happy Library people skills above, Bertha changed the High-Turnover-in-Staff Library into the Library with a Staff Waiting List. She led by organizing and then implementing the following strategic plan:

1. She discussed why they opened their library doors each day. The responses helped to define their mission and philosophy. "There really is no trick to developing an organizational culture or an organizational philosophy. It simply means recognizing the plain fact that measurable, quantifiable techniques of control are helpful but incomplete, and that, if the equally important but more subtle goals of the organization are not expressed openly through a philosophy, then numbers will rule, to the detriment of the organization."[6]
2. The processes involved in maintaining this mission determined the daily operating goals, that is, the functions that needed to be done. Necessary functions were providing trained personnel at each service desk; selecting, ordering, and processing resources; preparing interlibrary loans for requests not in the collection; and so forth. These policies and procedures had to be defined and consistently implemented. Staff members were encouraged to ask questions and receive additional training as needed. The knowledge level of the staff increased tremendously.
3. Staff members understood the library's objectives, that is, the focused and clearly defined activities that needed to be accomplished for the goals to be implemented.
4. Bertha explained the importance of surveying the people who used the library by asking, "What are your information needs?" During this needs assessment process, nonusers in the community were also surveyed. It was important to learn why they weren't using the library. Both sets of responses were important. This feedback provided an opportunity to confirm that their mission statement was aligned with their users' needs. They set the course of actions for future improve-

ments that would be made to the library's services and resources. These became the Library with a Staff Waiting List's strategic initiatives.

5. As the answers to these processes were unfolding, Bertha had a vision that depicted the future at the Library with a Staff Waiting List. She shared this enlightenment at a staff meeting so that the library team could brainstorm their thoughts and perceptions of her vision.

6. After additional meetings with discussions about the vision, mission, goals, objectives, and strategic initiatives, everyone shared their perceptions of the strengths, weaknesses, opportunities, and threats (SWOTs) of the factors involved within each element of this strategic plan.

7. Then Bertha's work really began. Based on the feedback from the library users, the nonusers, and the library team, she prepared a new organizational chart. The purpose of each position and job description focused on achieving the vision, mission, operating goals and objectives, and strategic initiatives. The chain of command for all library personnel was clearly defined. The level of authority was aligned with the decision-making processes, according to Drucker's principle that "while the effective decision itself is based on the highest level of conceptual understanding, the action commitment should be as close as possible to the capabilities of the people who have to carry it out."[7] After some tweaking as Drucker advises, everyone knew what his or her responsibilities and tasks were. Gantt charts were used so that everyone knew who was responsible for what tasks and when they would be done.[8]

8. From a library management perspective, this new document also clearly displayed what the staff could expect and how their performance would be measured. A new continuous performance appraisal system began with the concept of an incident file. When a supervisor observed an accomplishment that exceeded expectations, it would be documented. If/when an employee performed below expectation, not only would it be documented, but the supervisor would provide guidance and/or training for improvement in that area. Periodic reviews would occur as needed to confirm the staff member's performance improvement or to initiate necessary disciplinary actions. If dismissal became the next step, the incident file would provide clear documentation that the supervisor offered the staff member the appropriate training and assistance for legal purposes. There should be no surprises at evaluation time.

Bertha's strategy was to position those who thrived on change on the front lines, while those who resisted change could "hold the fort" as the environment was transitioning around them.

ERROR 3: CHANGE

Two Extremes Causing Opposite Mistakes

Library manager Nick was ready to retire. His mind was on his future travel plans. He did not take an interest in his employees, nor did he challenge them to improve. Consequently, the employees did not grow professionally, nor were they motivated to work. The library became the Status Quo Library.

When Nick retired from the Status Quo Library, library manager Henry was hired. He was the opposite. He assumed that every staff member wanted to grow professionally. He was frustrated that all employees didn't want to exceed expectations. He expected every staff member to belong to a library association, attend conferences, learn new skills, and share them with other staff members when he or she returned from conferences. This was a new philosophy that the staff didn't buy into at . . . you probably guessed it, Resistance-to-Change Library!

Solution

Super library manager Leonard came to the rescue. Leonard had management training via workshops at the Association of College and Research Libraries conferences, so he knew that some people would always resist change, and yet he remembered that change is constant. Consequently, he decided to implement the following strategies:

1. He would be flexible and embrace change by encouraging staff to benefit from their strengths. For example, new electronic databases usually require technical and public service support. Leonard let the staff select which function they would like to be assigned. If two employees requested the same task, they agreed to take different tasks and reverse their roles in the future.
2. He would encourage both collaborative and independent skills. Leonard observed that some staff members work effectively in teams, while others are more productive and creative working alone. He tried to create the right path for each person so that the staff members would enjoy their jobs and the library users would benefit too.
3. He would realize that lifelong learning equals a lifetime of learning. Effective library staff members, whether in a managerial role or being managed, should always be learning. One duty of library managers should be to provide a variety of opportunities for that learning to take place in a variety of venues and styles so that each staff member can find an approach in keeping with his or her individual learning style.

4. He would understand that everyone can be a leader. Staff members are most productive when they are committed to their work and they enjoy what they are doing and learning. Staff members can lead from all levels of an organizational chart. The American Library Association website offers a detailed set of leadership traits.[9]

CONCLUSION

Just as in life, sometimes "makeovers" are needed to steer a library in the right direction, that is, toward its mission, or possibly to redefine its mission. This occurs because it is common for library managers and staff to get caught up in trying to make grandiose strategic initiatives a reality when in fact they need to succeed with their daily operational goals and objectives.

A visionary library manager leads the way by keeping people as the top priority and directing them down the right path so that, with appropriate training, education, and experience, they can maximize their productivity and motivate others.

As does life itself, work environments consist of people, strategies, and change. This chapter focused on library staffing, grievous managerial errors, successful strategies, and suggestions to implement change in a positive and productive way. These activities can be tied together via staff development, training, and evaluation.

Not only does each stakeholder group of people in a library (e.g., staff, management, Friends of the Library group members) bring a different perception to the table, but each person within each group has a unique perception. Since perceptions are what we need to manage to, each managerial situation is different.

A job well planned is a job half done, so plan ahead, manage strategically, and lead with common sense!

NOTES

1. David A. Baldwin and Robert L. Migneault, *Humanistic Management by Teamwork: An Organizational and Administrative Alternative for Academic Libraries.* (Englewood, Colo.: Libraries Unlimited, 1996).

2. Camila A. Alire, "Two Intriguing Practices to Library Management Theory: Common Sense and Humanistic Applications," *Library Administration and Management* 18, no. 1 (2004): 41.

3. Jodi Healy, "Google Newsletter for Librarians," Google, http://www.google.com/librariancenter/newsletter/0512.html (accessed June 8, 2007).

4. Kenneth Blanchard and Sheldon M. Bowles, *Raving Fans: A Revolutionary Approach to Customer Service* (New York: Morrow, 1993).

5. H. Igor Ansoff, *From Strategic Planning to Strategic Management* (New York: Wiley, 1976).

6. William G. Ouchi and Raymond L. Price, "Hierarchies, Clans, and Theory Z: A New Perspective on Organization Development," *Organizational Dynamics* 21, no. 4 (1993): 70.

7. Peter F. Drucker, "The Effective Decision," *Harvard Business Review* 45, no. 1 (1967): 92.

8. Henry L. Gantt, *Organizing for Work* (New York: Harcourt, Brace, and Howe, 1919; repr., Easton, Md.: Hive, 1973).

9. American Library Association, "Leadership Traits," http://www.ala.org/ala/mgrps/rts/nmrt/initiatives/ladders/traits/traits.cfm (accessed May 24, 2009).

5

Corporate Culture, Knowledge Management, and Libraries

If We Only Knew What We Know

Luann DeGreve

An academic library director in middle America faces a challenge. It is a challenge that every manager has faced or will face—the resignation, retirement, or passing of a key employee. This employee has worked in the library for many years performing a variety of tasks. Because this employee has been so effective, no one ever worried about what she did or how she did it. The work just got done. The director now is worried because he does not know what he does not know. He is worried about what will be lost in the transition and what he can do to minimize the impact of that lack of knowledge. The staff is anxious because they will have to fill in and train the replacement. But how does one train a replacement when the nuances of the job are unknown to all but the person who has done the job for so long?

Truthfully, the setting of the library does not matter in this scenario. The library could be located anywhere in the world. The library could be an academic, public, school, or special library. The challenge could be faced by a director at a small or large institution, the manager of a large department, or the supervisor of one person. The challenge is the same—how does one learn what is held in the data collected by each department, what is held in the stories behind the processes of the department, and what is held in the working knowledge of the employees? Attention to knowledge management would ease this transition.

Libraries are repositories of information. Librarians are experts at identifying, collecting, organizing, and retrieving information. Over time, the tools used by librarians have changed. Yet the fundamental basis of what librarians do has not changed. Even though librarians are recognized as information experts, they often are not very skilled at knowledge management. On

39

the surface, information management and knowledge management appear to be the same. Yet they are different from one another. Guy St. Clair defines information management as "the organizational methodology that is concerned with the acquisition, arrangement, storage, retrieval, and use of information to produce knowledge."[1] Knowledge management, on the other hand, is "the process through which organizations extract value from their intellectual assets."[2] Information management is concerned with data, the raw materials of information. Knowledge management is concerned with the nuances of how decisions are made, what is hidden in the minds of the employees. The difference may be subtle, but it is very important. Knowledge management is important for the growth and survival of every organization. Those who are proactively managing an organization's knowledge base are poised to lead, while those who do not actively manage the organization's knowledge are prone to repeat the same mistakes.

BACKGROUND INFORMATION
ON KNOWLEDGE MANAGEMENT

Four Components of the Information Continuum

While much has been written in the management and library science literature on knowledge management, it is a good idea to review some of the fundamental principles on which knowledge management is based. This section will examine the makeup of the information continuum, the types of knowledge, and the role of corporate culture. More detailed information can be found in the sources cited in the notes at the end of this chapter.

The information continuum is made up of four components, each of which builds upon the others. The starting point is data. Data consists of the observations, facts, and figures collected by individuals. In libraries, these would include the number of people entering the library, a list of items purchased and their corresponding costs and use, the number of items processed by the technical services staff, and so forth. As data is organized for a specific purpose, it becomes information. The number of people entering the library is data. When the number of people entering the library is broken down by the day and hour, it becomes information. The number of items processed is data. The number of items processed per person each week is information. When information is analyzed, it becomes knowledge. "Knowledge is an elusive and complex process that requires an individual to make value judgments based on prior experiences and understanding of the patterns."[3] Examining the number of people entering the library during a given day or hour in the course of the year shows that there is a pattern of heavy traffic during the middle of the day. The number of items processed per person on a weekly basis shows that the staff is not able to keep up with the numbers of items coming into the library. Examining the list of items purchased and their usage shows that there is a great demand for materials on a particular subject. Wisdom, the final stage of the process, is the "ability and willingness to apply knowledge."[4] Wisdom is making a decision on how to use the knowledge. Heavy traffic times require additional staff at service points. Either the workflow in technical services needs to be redesigned or additional staff are needed to keep the items moving through the cataloging process. Greater demand for a particular subject requires more materials to be made available on the topic. There are subtle differences as one moves along the continuum. It is the action taken by a person at each level of the continuum that makes the difference. Data itself cannot suggest anything, but organizing data, analyzing it, and deciding what to do with it leads to wisdom.

Four Components of Knowledge Management

Knowledge management has four key components. These components are knowledge, management, information technology, and corporate culture. Each of these components affects the success of knowledge management.

"Knowledge is the 'knowing' embedded in people's experiences, skills, competencies, capabilities, talents, thoughts, ideas, ways of working, intuitions, and imaginations that manifests itself in the form of tangible artifacts, work processes, and routines in an organization."[5] There are two types of knowledge—explicit and tacit. Explicit knowledge is knowledge that has been transcribed in some format.[6] Each library that has written down its policies regarding library access, loan periods, collection development, emergency response and recovery, and so forth has contributed to the organization's knowledge. Detailed instructions on acquisitions and cataloging procedures, circulation procedures, and instructional goals further contribute to an organization's knowledge base. Having these types of explicit knowledge artifacts available will help anyone new coming into the library to learn about the organization.

Tacit knowledge is "the expertise and assumptions that individuals develop over the years that may never have been recorded or documented."[7] The library has a documented policy that users must come to the library to pick up their interlibrary loan materials; however, a certain category of users have their materials automatically mailed to them. This is not documented anywhere. It is a part of tradition. The history of the decision is held by the interlibrary loan manager and is unknown to the rest of the staff. The library wants to implement an information literacy campaign. The relationships built by the instruction librarian over the years help to begin the process of creating change. Without this key employee and her instincts and knowledge of the faculty, the library would have a more difficult time making this change. Tacit knowledge represents roughly 80 percent of the most important knowledge.[8] Without this knowledge, many library activities would not run very smoothly. It is vital that managers learn how to tap into the tacit knowledge of their employees.

According to Rob Cross and Lloyd Baird, there are five resources that serve as an organization's memory. The most important resource is what is in the minds of the employees. The second resource is explicit and tacit knowledge. Third, organizations create knowledge repositories based on the explicit knowledge that has been documented. Fourth, organizational memory is contained in processes. Fifth, memories are found in the products and services of the organization.[9] Each resource builds upon the others. The knowledge held in the minds of the employees is tacit knowledge, which can be tapped and converted into explicit knowledge. Processes can be documented. The reasons behind the development of products and services can be converted into explicit knowledge. The explicit knowledge of the organization can be communicated with others through the use of knowledge repositories. Creating, maintaining, and accessing each of these types of resources will aid in knowledge management.

A second component of knowledge management is management of explicit and tacit knowledge. The management of explicit knowledge requires organizations to create knowledge. Next, the knowledge must then be organized and made accessible to others. Employees have to use and apply the knowledge to a variety of circumstances. Tacit knowledge has to be managed also. One way to accomplish this is to convert it into explicit knowledge. The conversion can take place in a variety of ways including written communication, oral histories, hands-on instruction, training, and mentoring.[10]

Information technology, the third component, plays a supporting role in knowledge management. It is not a driving force; instead, information technology is used to create, organize, and retrieve knowledge. It does not add to the knowledge base itself. Technology has made the sharing of knowledge faster and easier in many respects. Technology can be used to create knowledge repositories to store organizational knowledge, which can be tapped by others working on similar problems. Technology can be used to create intranets or other types of internal networks where individuals can share information and knowledge without fear of theft. Technology has allowed for ease of communication and shared collaboration through e-mail, wikis, blogs, and so forth. All of this can contribute to the management of an organizational knowledge base.

The most important component of knowledge management is an open corporate culture. Schein defines corporate culture as "the pattern of basic assumptions that a given group has invented, discovered, or developed in learning to cope with its problems of external adaptation and internal integration, and that have worked well enough to be considered valid, and, therefore, to be taught to new members as the correct way to perceive, think, and feel in relation to those problems."[11] Creating a culture where individuals are encouraged to share knowledge must be one of the leading goals for a library. Managing organizational knowledge will fail if a culture does not value the sharing of information among its employees for it is destined to repeat the same mistakes and re-create the wheel over and over again.

Goman found there are five leading reasons employees give for not sharing information. They have a perception that knowledge is power. An employee who holds a piece of knowledge can wield power over someone who needs that knowledge. Second, people are insecure about the value of their knowledge. This can happen at a variety of levels within the organization. As a result, it is important for the manager to encourage everyone to contribute and to model that everyone has value. Third, people do not trust their coworkers. This is particularly true when people are placed together on cross-functional teams. It takes time to build trust within a team or group. Fourth, employees are afraid of negative consequences of sharing information. What seems, at first, to be an unpopular or wacky idea could really be the insight that was needed to move the group onward, but if the idea is not shared because of fear of the reaction, that forward movement does not occur. Finally, employees model what they see. If they work for managers who do not share information, then they are less likely to share what they know with others.[12]

Carla O'Dell and C. Jackson Grayson list five additional reasons why employees do not share information. First, organizations promote "silo" behavior where each department has its own goals and objectives and, therefore, focuses solely on its own needs. This can be seen in a library where the reference librarians are unaware of what the instruction librarians are teaching students, where the catalogers are not aware of how students access information, or where interlibrary loan personnel do not communicate a growing demand for specific materials to the collection development personnel. Each group is working solely on its own needs. Sharing the knowledge they are gaining could ease their workloads in the long run. Second, organizations value individual expertise more than sharing. Reward systems revolve around an individual's contribution to the organization and his or her accomplishments. Sharing of information does not always rate high in comparison. Third, people are not able to develop relationships across the organization. If a person does not know someone and has not developed a level of trust in that individual, it is unlikely that knowledge will be shared between the two. Fourth, the organization places an emphasis on documenting policies and procedures. It fails to account for the nuances of a task, the special circumstances that cause a person to deviate from the policy or procedure. Finally, organizations can be so goal-oriented that they fail to understand the time it takes to learn something new and to share that with others. If learning and sharing are not valued and rewarded, employees are less likely to commit themselves to those activities.[13]

BASIC STEPS TO KNOWLEDGE MANAGEMENT

Now, what does all this mean for the manager who has lost a key employee? The most damaging thing to knowledge management is having employees who are unwilling to learn and to share knowledge. It is up to the manager to create an environment where learning and sharing are encouraged, valued, and rewarded. Creating an open organizational culture is the first step a manager can take to help ease the loss of knowledge during a personnel transition. Changing an organization's culture is not easy, but the long-term benefits should serve as encouragement to stay the course. In "Successfully Managing and Executing Change," Ken Simonelic identifies eight things a manager needs to do to create successful and lasting change. A manager must create a sense of urgency for a change to occur. If change is not viewed as urgent, then other things that are considered more urgent can get in the way. Senior administrators must buy into the need for change. Senior administrators must model the change language and behavior for the idea to sink into the minds of the employees. The manager must have a clear vision, routinely communicate the vision, and remove any obstacles that get in the way of employees focusing on the vision. An unclear vision that is not communicated demonstrates to employees its lack of importance. Short-term wins must be celebrated. While celebrating the short-term wins, it is important not to declare change completed too soon. Finally, the organizational culture will change.[14]

Creating this new open culture will encourage people's willingness to learn new things and to share what they have learned. Employees will see that they are all on the same team, working together to achieve the same goals and vision. There is no longer a need to hoard information and knowledge to prove a person's value. The sharing of knowledge will be the new value of the employee. As more people have access to the thought processes behind decisions, the less likely it will be that important information will be lost when a person leaves the team.

Informal and formal conversations are one way this knowledge sharing can take place. Cross-training is another method that can be used to transfer this tacit knowledge. This can be particularly useful in smaller libraries where there is only one person doing a given task. Training a second person in the nuances of a given job will ensure there is someone else who can take over during an absence, fill in if additional help is needed, or assist with training a new person for the position. If cross-training is done well, then the loss of key knowledge should be minimized.

Another thing managers can do to prevent the loss of knowledge is to have all policies and procedures documented. To employees who have many other things to do, this might seem like an unnecessary exercise and a waste of time. However, for anyone who has started in a new position or had to take over for someone because of an emergency, having documented policies and procedures to follow can ease the transition. Having said that, merely having documentation is not enough. People have to be willing to read through the documentation as a part of training. Having people ignore what is right in front of them can demoralize those who took the time and effort to write everything down. It can also lead to a new employee's wasting valuable amounts of time re-creating the wheel when he or she should be building upon what is already in place.

Developing a set of best practices is a final thing that can be done to manage an organization's knowledge. "Many companies save millions of dollars by taking existing knowledge and applying it to similar situation [*sic*] elsewhere."[15] This can be knowledge management at its best. Best practices can be developed by any employee within an organization. Best practices can be learned through conversations with colleagues, professional reading, workshops, and conference attendance. It takes some level of courage to admit that an organization, department, or person is not doing a task in the smartest, most productive, or most efficient manner possible. Once the admittance is made, though, it becomes a matter of taking knowledge developed by someone else and applying it to the current situation. This brings the organization to the end of the information continuum and to wisdom.

CONCLUSION

Implementing a good knowledge management system first requires a manager to realize that the organization is missing key pieces of knowledge, preferably before the knowledge is needed. The second step is to identify what knowledge needs to be collected and how it should be collected. Organization and retrieval of the knowledge make up the third step of the process. Finally, having employees actively use and update the knowledge base will keep it robust. Overshadowing this process is the need for managers to value and reward the contributions and knowledge of their employees. This may seem like an oversimplification of the process, but at a fundamental level, this is all there is. People can get caught up in the details of how to accomplish each step. There is a large body of literature available to provide the details of each step of the process.

Implementing knowledge management in an organization produces a number of positive outcomes. Christina Stoll found that implementing knowledge management in her organization reduced staff time spent searching for information, reduced duplication of work, provided for more efficient customer service, provided more time for improving service, and created a better organization and use of institutional knowledge.[16] With these positive outcomes available, what is stopping your organization from developing a knowledge management system?

NOTES

1. Guy St. Clair, "Knowledge Services: Your Company's Keys to Performance Excellence," *Information Outlook* 5, no. 6 (June 2001): 8.

2. Simone Kaplan, "KM the Right Way," *CIO*, July 15, 2002, 76.

3. David C. Blair, "Knowledge Management: Hype, Hope, or Help?" *Journal of the American Society for Information Science and Technology* 53, no. 12 (October 2002): 1021.

4. Anthea Stratigos, "Knowledge Management Meets Future Information Users," *Online* 25, no. 1 (January/February 2001): 66.

5. Smiti Gandhi, "Knowledge Management and Reference Services," *Journal of Academic Librarianship* 30, no. 5 (September 2004): 370.

6. Claire McInerney, "Knowledge Management and the Dynamic Nature of Knowledge," *Journal of the American Society for Information Science and Technology* 53, no. 12 (October 2002): 1012.

7. McInerney, "Knowledge Management and Dynamic Nature," 1011.

8. David Stamps, "Is Knowledge Management a Fad?" *Training* 36, no. 4 (March 1999): 40.

9. Rob Cross and Lloyd Baird, "Technology Is Not Enough: Improving Performance by Building Organizational Memory," *Sloan Management Review* 41, no. 3 (Spring 2000): 70.

10. Gandhi, "Knowledge Management and Reference Services," 371.

11. Edgar H. Schein, "Coming to a New Awareness of Organizational Culture," *Sloan Management Review* 25, no. 2 (Winter 1984): 3.

12. Carol Kinsey Goman, "Five Reasons People Don't Tell What They Know," *portalKMOL*, 2002, http://www.kmol.online.pt.artigos/200212/gom02_e.html (accessed March 9, 2007).

13. Carla O'Dell and C. Jackson Grayson, "If Only We Know What We Know," *California Management Review* 40, no. 3 (Spring 1998): 157.

14. Ken Simonelic, "Successfully Managing and Executing Change," *Journal of Business Forecasting* 25, no. 3 (Fall 2006): 20.

15. Maitrayee Ghosh and Ashok Jambekar, "Networks, Digital Libraries and Knowledge Management: Trends & Developments," *DESIDOC Bulletin of Information Technology* 23, no. 5 (September 2003): 9.

16. Christina Stoll, "Writing the Book on Knowledge," *Association Management* 56, no. 4 (April 2004): 58.

BIBLIOGRAPHY

Blair, David C. "Knowledge Management: Hype, Hope, or Help?" *Journal of the American Society for Information Science and Technology* 53, no. 12 (October 2002): 1019–28.

Cross, Rob, and Lloyd Baird. "Technology Is Not Enough: Improving Performance by Building Organizational Memory." *Sloan Management Review* 41, no. 3 (Spring 2000): 69–78.

Gandhi, Smiti. "Knowledge Management and Reference Services." *Journal of Academic Librarianship* 30, no. 5 (September 2004): 368–81.

Ghosh, Maitrayee, and Ashok Jambekar. "Networks, Digital Libraries and Knowledge Management: Trends & Developments." *DESIDOC Bulletin of Information Technology* 23, no. 5 (September 2003): 3–11.

Goman, Carol Kinsey. "Five Reasons People Don't Tell What They Know." *portalKMOL.* 2002. http://www.kmol.online.pt.artigos/200212/gom02_e.html (accessed March 9, 2007).

Kaplan, Simone. "KM the Right Way." *CIO,* July 15, 2002, 74–81.

McInerney, Claire. "Knowledge Management and the Dynamic Nature of Knowledge." *Journal of the American Society for Information Science and Technology* 53, no. 12 (October 2002): 1009–18.

O'Dell, Carla, and C. Jackson Grayson. "If Only We Know What We Know." *California Management Review* 40, no. 3 (Spring 1998): 154–74.

Schein, Edgar H. "Coming to a New Awareness of Organizational Culture." *Sloan Management Review* 25, no. 2 (Winter 1984): 3–16.

Simonelic, Ken. "Successfully Managing and Executing Change." *Journal of Business Forecasting* 25, no. 3 (Fall 2006): 20–21.

Stamps, David. "Is Knowledge Management a Fad?" *Training* 36, no. 4 (March 1999): 36–42.

St. Clair, Guy. "Knowledge Services: Your Company's Key to Performance Excellence." *Information Outlook* 5, no. 6 (June 2001): 6–12.

Stoll, Christina. "Writing the Book on Knowledge." *Association Management* 56, no. 4 (April 2004): 56–63.

Stratigos, Anthea. "Knowledge Management Meets Future Information Users." *Online* 25, no. 1 (January/February 2001): 65–67.

Swartz, Nikki. "The 'Wonder Years' of Knowledge Management." *Information Management Journal* 37, no. 3 (May/June 2003): 53–57.

Townley, Charles T. "Knowledge Management and Academic Libraries." *College & Research Libraries* 62, no. 1 (January 2001): 44–55.

6

Knowing the Library User

Harvey R. Gover

A FAILED TECHNOLOGY INITIATIVE

About seven years ago, the director of distance learning library services and the head of reference for a midsized state-supported university in the upper midwestern United States both learned about chat reference at a conference. Enthusiastically impressed about the certainty of patron buy-in for this new type of service, the two convinced their library management team and their respective departments that the software should be purchased, training scheduled, and a joint service set up to be operated together by the two departments. A large monetary investment was made, the training was conducted, and the two departments with very different missions undertook to serve each other's patrons. Even so, very little response to the chat reference option was received from those patrons. With only about one hundred transactions in the first year and a half, most of which came from main-campus students who did not want to walk from their workstations in the library to the reference desk to seek help, the service was shut down, leaving nothing to show for what turned out to be a sizable investment of money, time, and personnel.

Other than the procedures described above, little else had been done to ensure the acceptance and use of the newly introduced technology. No surveys had been made to determine the potential need and receptivity for this technology. No advance communication had been sent out to potential users before installing the chat reference. No introductory communication was sent out right after making the chat reference available, except for placing news blurbs on the home pages for the main library and the distance learning library services unit. Some well-attended introductory sessions were provided teaching faculty to offer chat as an instructional tool option, but little actual use resulted. No additional promotional activities were undertaken, nor were any additional promotional communications provided directly to patrons when it became evident that the service was not being well used. A press release was sent out from the university communications office, but no news outlet picked it up. No feedback was sought after shutting down the service to learn why neither the on-campus nor the distance learning students had wanted to use it. The assumption was made that the largely older distance learning students had preferred the traditional phone and e-mail contact long provided by the distance learning library services unit. The on-campus students had the option of seeking help in person from library personnel, though ironically, as noted, their use of the chat option within the library to contact staff right there was its primary use. Finally, the chat option itself was found to be inefficient and not to work well on standard phone lines. With this observation comes the admonition to know the technology as well as the user. No postconference follow-up investigation of the technology had been done to confirm or refute its effectiveness before making a final decision on whether to adopt it.

THE GROWING CHALLENGES

As this hypothetical scenario of a failed chat reference initiative so vividly portrays, knowing today's users of academic libraries is an increasingly challenging undertaking. Students are more diverse in age, in their cultural origins, and in their generational characteristics. Anticipating whether and how users of academic libraries will use existing and possible additional library services and materials is rendered ever more complex, not only by this increasing diversity among groups of users, but also by the unique and often unpredictable characteristics of individual users. Two emerging areas of study, technology acceptance and needs assessment, have proven useful, and recent publications relating to them will be introduced. A third approach focuses on defining student characteristics by a variety of social science research methods.

Predicting whether and how library patrons will actually use specific resources is rather like playing *Wheel of Fortune*. One might even be tempted to quip, "Russian roulette!" For example, when e-books were first developed and libraries began collecting them, it was anticipated that library patrons would use them primarily to read "from cover to cover" as substitutes for print books. However, a study by Edward W. Walton, the acting dean of university libraries at Southwest Baptist University in Bolivar, Missouri, indicated that students prefer to use e-books strictly as sources for specific research topics and employed the internal searching capability to find and use only passages relevant to their topic needs. If a book was to be used for more than a quick search and retrieval of relevant passages, students preferred to have and use a print copy of the book, if available.[1]

One must also take care not to make assumptions based upon stereotypic generational expectations. Kelly Heyboer of the *Chicago Tribune* reports on the initial, surprising results, too new to have made it into the professional literature, of a new online exam from the Educational Testing Service, the Information and Communication Technology Literacy Assessment, or ICT. The new exam was piloted among 6,300 college and university students across the nation. Students were not nearly as adept at online skills as had been generally assumed and expected.

> Just 52 percent could correctly judge the objectivity of a Web site and only 65 percent assessed the site's authoritativeness. When asked to use a search engine to look for information on the Internet, only 40 percent entered multiple search terms to narrow the results. Test takers also had trouble figuring out when it is ethical to use information they find on the Internet in their own work and how to rewrite the facts they find at Web sites for a new audience.[2]

That such skills are not entirely intuitive and are not universally held by members of the "net generation," or any other age group, is becoming rapidly evident with implications for both administrative and information literacy instruction decisions in academic libraries. An early conclusion from the initial testing is that these skills will need to be taught as a whole new discipline, no surprise for academic librarians. For how many decades, now, has this been the core message of information literacy librarians?

MEASURING TECHNOLOGY ACCEPTANCE

A number of technology acceptance studies have provided valuable insights using the Technology Acceptance Model (TAM), first developed in the late 1980s by Fred D. Davis at the University of Michigan, Ann Arbor.[3] The TAM uses perceived usefulness and perceived ease of use as indicators of user acceptance of information technology. Literally hundreds of studies, some published as professional journal articles and others prepared as doctoral dissertations, have been prepared using the TAM. A selected number of recent studies that employ the TAM or extended models of it, and thereby provide techniques useful for learning more about library users, will be identified and some of their findings noted. Also included in this section are two closely related studies that do not employ the TAM.

As of this writing, the most recent of the TAM studies, prepared by Susan K. Lippert of Drexel University and John A. Volkmar of Otterbein College, integrates the Theory of Reasoned Action (TRA) and the TAM with Hofstede's

Masculinity/Femininity (MAS/FEM) work value dimension. Their cross-cultural study focuses on

> post adoption attitudes and behaviors among a mixed gender sample of 366 United States and Canadian users of a specialized supply chain IT. We test 11 hypotheses about attitudes towards IT within and between subgroups of users classified by nationality and gender. Consistent with the national MAS/FEM scores and contrary to the conventional consideration of the U.S. and Canada as a unitary homogenous cultural unit, we found significant differences between U.S. men and women, but not between Canadian men and women. These results support the importance of the MAS/FEM dimension—independent of gender—on user attitudes and help to clarify the relationship between culture and gender effects. . . . The integration of TRA with TAM as the theoretical grounding for this study is employed because the use of these theories provides the most comprehensive structure to understand technology adoption. Additionally, TRA has consistently been found to be an effective baseline theory for addressing technology acceptance.[4]

Andy Borchers of Kettering University explores more than five years of institution-wide updating and development of IT at a small, and otherwise unidentified, midwestern urban university. Borchers's study reports on one use of the TAM and demonstrates the importance of departmental planning that takes into account what is happening across an entire campus, covering 1997 through 2003 at Watkins University, a fictional name used in Borchers's report. Both faculty and student acceptance or rejection of existing and proposed campus IT developments are explored and explained within their institutional context and predominant student characteristics.[5]

Susan Elwood of the College of Education at the Texas A&M University regional campus in Corpus Christi, and Chuleeporn Changchit and Robert Cutshall of the College of Business there, used an extension of the TAM in their investigation of student perceptions of a laptop initiative. The TAM was expanded using a third factor, perceived change. Their study produced a survey tool suitable for use at other universities and with other technologies.

> Based on the results of this study, the new factor, perceived change, suggests that universities educate students on the changes accompanying the implementation of a laptop program. The more knowledge the students have about positive changes a laptop program can lead to, the greater chance they will support such a program. . . . The three factors (perceived usefulness, perceived ease of use, and perceived change) can play a major role in determining the acceptance of a laptop initiative. These results appear to be contributing factors to technology acceptance and warrant further investigation. Future research should include faculty, staff, and administrators before any generalizations can be made.[6]

These principles can apply to any IT initiative in a university setting, including academic libraries.

Three educational research specialists from the University of Georgia system, Libby V. Morris, Catherine Finnegan, and Sz-Shyan Wu, measured student performance in online courses using student data and statistical analysis. Technology acceptance was not measured, so it could not be correlated with student achievement, although the study might have been far more valuable had technology acceptance been included. The same elements necessary for student success in traditional course formats were shown to be factors corresponding with success in online courses: frequency of contact with course materials, amount of time spent online using course materials, apparent willingness to engage in repetition, and apparent motivation based upon frequency of contact and length of time spent with course materials.[7] Prior to the kinds of tracking enabled through student use of online course resources, such direct measures of student involvement with course materials were not possible. When available, circulation records for reserve materials were one partial exception, but such statistics did not always track individual use of specific items.

M. D. Sankey of the University of Southern Queensland, Australia, "reports on research investigating the perceptions of first year distance education students studying a foundation communications course using a multimodal learning environment. It demonstrates higher levels of engagement are possible when a neomillennial learning approach is adopted for designing course materials catering to a diverse student body, whilst maintaining a more balanced environment for more traditional learners."[8] Sankey describes an initiative to add online and other enhanced course materials to an existing distance learning program of the university. Traditional print options were maintained along with the newly offered CD and online ones. The course designers undertook to offer choices for as many different learning styles and generational preferences as possible.

> Clearly, further research into this form of delivery is required. . . . It is hoped that the findings of this study may encourage more educators to consider the adoption of technology for the purpose of designing and delivering distance education courses, starting at a first year level. However, in doing so, there are important issues relating to how the implementation of these new technologies can be best integrated before the full benefits to the learning community can be realised.[9]

An additional courseware study, undertaken by Brett J. L. Landry, Rodger Griffeth, and Sandra Hartman of the Department of Management at the University of New Orleans, used the TAM to examine student perceptions of Blackboard, as a means of web-enhanced instruction (WEI). According to the researchers, WEI

> is not intended to replace the traditional classroom setting, but rather to supplement the traditional lecture with course content that can be accessed

from campus or the Internet. . . . This study provided findings in several areas. First, it considered whether the TAM could be extended from IS [information systems] and acceptance of technology among IS users to students and WEI in the academic setting. Results from this research suggest that the TAM is appropriate for the academic setting and, specifically, that it represents a useful instrument for measuring student reactions to Blackboard, the WEI tool used in this study. Additionally, however, perceptions of Blackboard elements do not receive equal acceptance. Instead, students have very different perceptions about the Usefulness and, as a result, the Usage of Blackboard features. The features that are part of the Course Content factor are used more often and are perceived as more Useful than those items that provide Course Support and communication.[10]

Another extended model of the TAM was used by Sheryl L. Shivers-Blackwell of the School of Business and Industry at Florida A&M University and Atira C. Charles, then a PhD student in organizational behavior at Arizona State University, to test students' readiness to accept a new technology in an academic setting. In their theoretical model, Gender, Computer Self-Efficacy, Perceived Benefits of the New Technology, Readiness for Change, Attitude Toward Usage, and Intent to Use were added to the TAM's Perceived Ease of Use and Perceived Usefulness.

An organizational implication of this research is that an individual's readiness for change is an important factor when implementing a new technology. Organizational investments in technology must take into account more than the financial costs of that technology, they must be sensitive to user characteristics. Subsequently, knowledge of individual differences (i.e. demographics, values, beliefs) among technology users is an important component that should shape the strategic, legal, economic and operational considerations that decision makers must understand when implementing a new technology. The leadership of an organization should address individual differences that may influence their member's [sic] readiness for change. For example, this research has shown that an individual's gender and their [sic] perception of . . . benefits are significantly related to readiness for change, and that computer self-efficacy is related to attitude toward usage and one's intent to use. Further research should examine additional individual-level factors in order to assist in the effective implementation.[11]

A study by Ya-Ching Lee of the Institute of Communication Management at National Sun Yat-Sen University, Taiwan, further confirmed the value of an extended TAM in surveying student acceptance of a new e-learning system (ELS) in both mandatory and voluntary settings. In the extended TAM, "competing behavioral intentions" refers to a set of alternatives, including the ELS, the others of which compete with the ELS for the user's choice. The decision to adopt the ELS in opposition to the other choices is considered a positive decision. "Subjective norm" is determined by whether "salient social referents" think an individual should or should not engage in a particular behavior. "Perceived network externality" refers to "an increase in the value of a product or service to a consumer, not because of the inherent quality of the product or service, but because of increasing numbers of others adopting it."

> The extended TAM for an ELS, incorporating the notion of competing behavioral intention, content quality, computer self-efficacy, perceived network externality, course attributes and subjective norm, provides a detailed account of the key forces underpinning decision making with regard to ELS adoption, explaining up to 54 percent of the variance in this important driver of usage intentions. . . . Moreover, this extended TAM shows that perceived network externality exerts a significant direct effect on usage intentions, perceived usefulness and perceived ease of use.[12]

With direct managerial implications for libraries, a study of web-based subscription database acceptance reported by Jong-Ae Kim of Dongbu Information Technology, Seoul, South Korea, uses another extended model of the TAM. The added elements included Subjective Norms, Job Relevance, Output Quality, Result Demonstrability, User Training, Accessibility, Terminology Clarity, and Intended Use. Intended Use refers to the decision to use the technology. "The results obtained from this study indicate that both perceived usefulness and ease of use are positively associated with intended use. The effect of usefulness beliefs on intended use was greater than the effect of ease of use beliefs."[13] Other positive influence was indicated by Job Relevance, Result Demonstrability, and Subjective Norm, with the strongest influence from Terminology Clarity.[14]

FOCUSING ON USER CHARACTERISTICS

So far, studies have been described that focused on users of particular technologies. The works in this section focus directly on the students and on defining their characteristics, including their interactions with technology, rather than looking exclusively at their uses of specific technologies. The first of these is *Educating the Net Generation*, an e-book by Diana G. Oblinger and James L. Oblinger.[15] I first became aware of *Educating the Net Generation* when reading M. D. Sankey's Australian study described earlier.[16] Sankey refers to a finding reported in *Educating the Net Generation* that these students do not necessarily prefer exclusively online course offerings to traditional classroom settings. More specifically, Sankey's reference was to a statement in the Oblingers' opening chapter, "Is It Age or IT: First Steps Toward Understanding the Net Generation":

> Since Net Geners spend so much of their time online, it seems reasonable to expect that they would have a strong preference for Web-based courses. The

reverse is actually true, as illustrated by a study from the University of Central Florida. Older students (Matures and Baby Boomers) are much more likely to be satisfied with fully Web-based courses than are traditional-age students. The reason relates to the Net Gen desire to be connected with people and to be social as well as their expectations of higher education. Traditional-age students often say they came to college to work with faculty and other students, not to interact with them online. Older learners tend to be less interested in the social aspects of learning; convenience and flexibility are much more important.[17]

Diana Oblinger works for EDUCAUSE, the online publisher of their online book, and James Oblinger works for North Carolina State University. *Educating the Net Generation* is a major work providing valuable observations for all postsecondary educators. As veteran educator Ines Eishen expressed in an e-mail to me on May 28, 2007, *"Educating the Net Generation should be mandatory reading for all distance teachers. Fascinating."*

The second work in this section, focusing directly on the students, is a conference paper in which Judi Briden, Vicki Burns, and Ann Marshall of the University of Rochester libraries report on a 2004–2006 interdisciplinary ethnographic study of how undergraduates on their campus do their work, including their use of technology and their involvement in campus life. The paper discusses

> how they use library resources, staff, and facilities in the process of writing research papers and completing research-based assignments for their college classes. In this paper, we report on the methods, findings, and programming outcomes of our Undergraduate Research Project. The Project has had a significant impact on our attitudes about our students, our understanding of the ways that students engage in academic work, the programs of the River Campus Libraries. . . . The Undergraduate Research Project was directed by Lead Anthropologist Nancy Fried Foster and a twelve-member project team. Project subteams for reference, facilities, and digital initiatives focused on specific questions and outcomes for these areas. During the Project, the teams used a variety of ethnographic methods including interviews, field observations, surveys, work-practice study, cultural probes, and design workshops.[18]

Participants in the Undergraduate Research Project were fascinated by both the process and the results. "One central finding was the importance of viewing our students' lives in their entirety: to see students, not just in terms of the library, but in a greater appreciation of students' full range of experiences. . . . Learning about students' routines helped us develop realistic views about how the library intersects with students' complicated lives."[19] Among the ongoing outcomes of the project was a significant change in the library's organizational culture, engendered by the enthusiasm for the project, with staff members becoming more open to making spontaneous changes than in the past. There was a redesign of printing in a large reference area. Student ideas from a series of design workshops within the project were later used in the planning of a major library renovation. In conjunction with the campus IT department, a new student portal was designed. Late-night reference services were instituted. When it was learned that students consult with their parents about their assignments, a breakfast introducing subject librarians was given as part of the parents' orientation. Projects for articulating on campus the function of reference librarians were undertaken, including the use of librarian-tutors in the Writing Center. Means for strengthening connections between faculty and their respective subject librarians were explored.[20]

ASSESSMENT

The lead resource for this section on assessment as a tool for gaining knowledge of academic library users is an article by Amos Lakos and Shelley Phipps on creating a culture of assessment in academic libraries. Lakos is a librarian at the Rosenfeld Management Library of the Anderson School of Management at the University of California, Los Angeles. Phipps is assistant dean for team and organization development at the University of Arizona, Tucson. In a research report that could easily serve as a prototype for framing a set of standards for assessment in academic libraries, Lakos and Phipps demonstrate that meeting the needs of library users involves far more than just assuming user characteristics, or even surveying user preferences, and requires building an entire culture of assessment across the whole library organization.

> Transforming our libraries to reflect a culture of assessment is essential to increasing our success with customers and stakeholders and maintaining relevancy in a competitive environment. Creating a culture of assessment pushes the organization to focus on understanding changing customer needs and on producing value-added outcomes for customers. . . . Developing a culture of assessment is about learning how to learn. It is about developing the organization's and the individual's learning capabilities. It necessitates curiosity. The new competence, experience, and learning agility that are part of the creation of a culture of assessment lead to new confidence and enhanced expertise. This new expertise leads to more effective and measurable outcomes for customers and stakeholders, which in turn heighten the potential for survival and relevancy in a competitive information service environment.[21]

User Surveys in College Libraries, compiled by Mignon S. Adams, then library director for Philadelphia College of Pharmacy and Science, and Jeffrey A. Beck, then reference and electronic resources librarian at Wabash College, provides historic background on assessment and other methods for surveying users of academic libraries. Numerous examples of survey instruments used in college libraries across the United States are included. The authors open by reporting the results of a survey of surveys in college libraries that launched their project. Covered are general surveys, surveys adapted from other sources, surveys of online services, surveys on specific areas of the library, facilities surveys, focus groups and interviews, and reports. A selected bibliography takes the reader to still further resources, many of which are landmark works.[22]

Xi Shi and Sarah Levy facilitate further research and the application of measurement instruments from other fields to assessment in academic libraries. Shi and Levy include an analysis of LibQUAL+, a service quality assessment tool for libraries, with suggestions for improvement based upon the original properties of its predecessor, SERVQUAL. "Recommendations are offered for better development of a research guided approach that can be used to identify refinements for more reliable measures and to steer practical assessment activities in libraries. Employing a research-guided approach allows libraries to evaluate their services systematically, identify any areas for improvement effectively, and thus manage their daily operations successfully."[23]

Indicative of the growth and influence of LibQUAL+ as an assessment tool for academic libraries, the following announcement was sent out via e-mail on May 17, 2007, to promote attendance at LibQUAL+ events at the 2007 annual conference of the American Library Association:

> LibQUAL+® Offers Five Events at ALA Annual Conference, Including Forum and Workshops.
>
> Washington, DC—The LibQUAL+® team announces the following events, scheduled in conjunction with the American Libraries Association (ALA) Annual Conference in Washington, DC, June 2007:

> #### LibQUAL+® Forum

> The LibQUAL+® Forum features A. "Parsu" Parasuraman speaking on measuring in-person and online library service quality in celebration of the 1,000 libraries that have implemented LibQUAL+®. Parsu is a highly sought-after speaker on service quality measurement. He is one of the key researchers in the marketing services field that established the methods used in the development of LibQUAL+®.

> #### LibQUAL+® 2007: An Introduction

> This workshop provides both current and prospective LibQUAL+® participants with information on the project's development and origins, as well as practical information on the process of implementing the survey at your institution. A buffet breakfast will be served.

LibQUAL+® Fifth Annual Share Fair

This informal (science-fair style) gathering features brief presentations/poster sessions by current and past LibQUAL+® survey participants highlighting examples of both quantitative and qualitative analysis available from survey results. The Share Fair also offers an opportunity to learn about other institutions' overall LibQUAL+® experience.

LibQUAL+® 2007 Community: A Results Meeting

The LibQUAL+® Results Meeting is aimed at library staff who participated in the 2007 Session I survey. The goals of this session are to (a) provide an overview of the latest round of LibQUAL+® participation, (b) report the latest research, (c) demonstrate best practices in using the results, and (d) engage participants in interpreting their institutional notebooks. Attendees will have the opportunity to ask questions related to the results, provide feedback on their survey experience, learn from other participants, and discuss how to put LibQUAL+® results into action. Please bring your LibQUAL+® notebooks if you have specific questions regarding your results.

Preparing to Work Effectively with LibQUAL+® Survey Results

This workshop will enable staff responsible for administering the LibQUAL+® survey to develop work plans that they can apply in their institutions in order to: organize their colleagues and committees to work with LibQUAL+®, perform some simple analyses of the results data, present the results effectively to various stakeholders, utilize data to target areas for improvement, and develop a process of continuous assessment. Please bring your LibQUAL+® notebooks. A buffet breakfast will be served.

About LibQUAL+®

LibQUAL+® is a suite of services that libraries use to solicit, track, understand, and act upon users' opinions of service quality. These services are offered to the library community by the Association of Research Libraries (ARL). The program's centerpiece is a rigorously tested Web-based survey bundled with training that helps libraries assess and improve library services, change organizational culture, and market the library.

LibQUAL+® is on the Web at http://www.libqual.org/.
For more information, contact:
Kristina Justh
Customer Relations Coordinator
Statistics & Measurement
Association of Research Libraries
kristina@arl.org
(202) 296-2296 ext. 136

Kaylyn Groves
Managing Editor, Web Content
Association of Research Libraries
21 Dupont Circle NW #800
Washington DC 20036
tel: 202.296.2296 x103
fax: 202.872.0884[24]

Just as a reference in Sankey's Australian study led to my discovery of the highly significant *Educating the Net Generation*, a search for additional, more recent publications by Amos Lakos led me to discover *Outcomes Assessment in Higher Education: Views and Perspectives*,[25] edited by Peter Hernon and Robert E. Dugan, via Lakos's 2005 review. Concerning the significance of *Outcomes Assessment in Higher Education*, Lakos stated,

> Reading this book would benefit all librarians, especially those engaged in information literacy. However, this book is especially a must read for academic library leaders and managers and all those who see the future of the library becoming more integrated in the learning process. The contents make a strong case for campus-wide collaboration for developing partnerships with faculty and other campus stakeholders for advancing student learning outcomes.[26]

Peter Hernon and Robert E. Dugan are both editors of and contributors to the collection of studies contained in *Outcomes Assessment in Higher Education*.[27] Peter Hernon is professor of library and information science at Simmons College, an expert on government information policy, and author of more than 240 works. Robert E. Dugan is library director at Suffolk University and the author of eight books and over fifty research articles. One of their contributors is Cecilia L. Lopez, who recounts a decade of institution-wide assessment development among member institutions of the Higher Education Commission of the North Central Association of Colleges and Schools from 1989 to 1999. "Today, the commission's vision is that all of its affiliated colleges and universities will recognize the value of becoming student-centered learning organizations committed to continuous improvement in the quality of the education achieved by their students."[28] Of special value to academic libraries are Lopez's descriptions of the activities and role of the campus assessment committee, since these are directly applicable to the work of an academic library assessment committee.[29] The accomplishments of the Washington State University Libraries Assessment Working Group, as presented on their website, are a primary example, with LibQUAL+ being a major focus.[30] Sarah K. McCord and Mary M. Nofsinger provided an earlier, more detailed report on the Libraries Assessment Working Group at the Washington State University libraries and the second pilot of LibQUAL+.[31]

Another contributor to *Outcomes Assessment in Higher Education*, Elizabeth W. Carter, describes a number of assessment initiatives undertaken by a college library at the Citadel:

> Perseverance in measuring the success of what one does, and the collection and analysis of useful data, can develop into greater support from administrators as they report college-wide assessment to governing and accreditation agencies. Such support may aid in continuing and expanding assessment efforts and to correcting problems exposed by assessment. Information gained from the Citadel Library's assessment projects has resulted in additional funding for more full-text databases and the creation of more and better-quality study areas. The assessment circle is closed when information is acted upon.[32]

In a chapter of *Outcomes Assessment in Higher Education* contributed by the editors, Hernon and Dugan, the two view assessment and evaluation from four different perspectives: those of the library/academic program, the institution, the user/customer, and the stakeholder.[33] They note:

> The library profession, and other groups, need to view the spectrum of measures from the four perspectives and to include relevant methodologies as part of their tool chest. Complicating matters, libraries and other institutional players may need guidance as they select from the various options. However, they should not be seduced into believing that measures applicable to the library-centered and institution-centered perspectives necessarily apply fully or adequately to the other two perspectives. The impact of outcomes assessment is only starting to unfold, and such assessment is intended to alter campus cultures over time. To be successful in an environment that increasingly focuses on accountability for excellence, academic libraries need to contribute broadly to student learning and to gain recognition for their successes. However, their contributions and successes will be linked to outcomes assessment and their ability to contribute to the development of educated individuals who become lifelong learners. Thus, any evidence gathered must demonstrate the development of students from the time of their entry into the program of study to their graduation: changes in behavior, knowledge, problem solving, critical thinking, and communication skills.[34]

THE FUTURE

Hernon and Dugan supplied quite an effective lead-in for a focus on the future. In a chapter of *Educating the Net Generation*, Chris Dede of Harvard University describes in some detail the electronic options currently available to students and how they are being used. Dede closes with projections for the institutional technology requirements and faculty development needs necessary for institutions of higher learning to succeed:

> Students of all ages with increasingly neomillennial learning styles will be drawn to colleges and universities that have these capabilities: *Wireless* everywhere—provide total coverage of the campus; subsidize uniform mobile wireless devices offering convergence of media (phone, PDA, gaming, Internet); *Multipurpose habitats*—creating layered/blended/personalizable places rather than specialized locations (such as computer labs); *Augmented reality*—experiment with smart objects and intelligent contexts (via GPS and RFID tags and transceivers); and *"Mirroring"*—experiment with virtual environments that replicate physical settings but offer "magical" capabilities for immersive experience.
>
> Four implications for investments in professional development also are apparent. Faculty will increasingly need capabilities in: *Co-design*—developing learning experiences students can personalize; *Co-instruction*—using knowledge sharing among students as a major source of content and pedagogy; *Guided social constructivist and situated learning pedagogies*—infusing case-based participatory simulations into presentational/assimilative instruction; and *Assessment beyond tests and papers*—evaluating collaborative, nonlinear, associational webs of representations; using peer-developed and peer-rated forms of assessment; employing student assessments to provide formative feedback on faculty effectiveness.[35]

Near the end of *Outcomes Assessment in Higher Education*, Hernon's "Preparing for the Future" chapter actually constitutes a beginning rather than an ending. All the necessary steps for getting started with assessment including cultural implications are outlined there, and a selected bibliography of introductory source material is included as a table within the text. Since Hernon's is not the last chapter in the book, the old formula of reading the first chapter and the last chapter before any others does not exactly apply here, but it certainly would not be inappropriate to make this one of the first chapters of the book that you read.[36]

In his bibliography of introductory source material in "Preparing for the Future," Hernon[37] includes an earlier work that he and Dugan coauthored, *An Action Plan for Outcomes Assessment in Your Library*.[38] Although "saving the best for last" was not my motivation for placing *An Action Plan* at the end of this chapter, one can certainly make a case for its being among the most important of the resources covered. For those exploring assessment options for their libraries, *An Action Plan* is an essential tool. Among the chapter topics are assessment plans, reports, and guides in institutions of higher learning; developing an assessment plan for measuring student learning outcomes; information literacy assessment efforts of some academic libraries; outcomes as a type of assessment; the research process; evidence demonstrating the achievement of outcomes; service quality and satisfaction; and making a commitment to accountability and learning outcomes assessment.

MOVING FORWARD

Shaping the future through knowing the library user has emerged as the theme of this chapter. The works described were chosen based upon the originality and significance of their contributions to increasing and improving the means by which academic librarians can better learn user characteristics and predict user needs. Criteria for choosing these works were of necessity highly selective. Comments concerning these works and the quotes chosen from them were intended to lead the reader to their full text and to additional works they recommend or reference. Together these works constitute a tool kit for moving forward in improving academic library services and materials in adaptation to rapidly evolving user needs. This chapter closes with a summary listing of a number of prescriptive statements that have appeared throughout the chapter.

SUMMARY OF PIVOTAL STATEMENTS

In order to give them additional emphasis and to increase their utility for the reader, the following statements have been lifted from the chapter text and arrayed here. Since sources were cited above, for simplicity and focus these statements are provided here without repeating quotation marks and citations.

These procedures and devices may be used to ensure the success of introducing a new technology:

- Use surveys to determine the potential need and receptivity for a new technology.
- Communicate in advance with users before installing a new technology.
- Provide introductory communication right after making a new technology available.
- Offer introductory training sessions after a new technology is made available.
- Institute additional promotional activities after a new technology is in place.
- Provide additional promotional communications directly to patrons after a new technology is in place.
- Issue media releases to expand communication before and after introduction of the new technology.
- Seek feedback on a technology that failed to receive acceptance.
- Know the technology as well as the users.

- Thoroughly investigate the performance of a proposed technology.
- Make no assumptions based upon stereotypic generational expectations.
- The Technology Acceptance Model (TAM), along with extended adaptations of it, provides techniques for learning more about library users and their potential for accepting a particular technology.
- Hofstede's Masculinity/Femininity (MAS/FEM) scores have been used to demonstrate a relationship between culture and gender effects in technology acceptance.
- Integration of the Theory of Reasoned Action (TRA) with the TAM and the MAS/FEM scores provides a comprehensive structure to understand technology adoption.
- Combine the institutional context with predominant student characteristics in exploring technology acceptance.
- The more knowledge students are supplied about a proposed technology, the more apt they are to accept it.
- Future research on technology acceptance should include faculty, staff, and administrators before any generalizations can be made.
- The same elements necessary for student success in traditional course formats are factors corresponding with success in online courses: frequency of contact with course materials, amount of time spent online using course materials, apparent willingness to engage in repetition, and apparent motivation based upon frequency of contact and length of time spent with course materials.
- Offer choices for as many different learning styles and generational preferences as possible.
- Realization of full benefits of implementation of new technologies depends upon their best integration.
- The TAM has been demonstrated to be appropriate for academic settings and a useful instrument for measuring student reactions to new technologies.
- An individual's readiness for change is an important factor when implementing a new technology.
- Organizational investments in technology must take into account more than the financial costs of that technology; they must be sensitive to user characteristics.
- Knowledge of individual differences (i.e., demographics, values, beliefs) among technology users is an important component.
- The leadership of an organization should address individual differences that may influence their members' readiness for change.
- "Net generation" students do not prefer online course offerings to traditional classroom settings; in fact, their preference is for traditional classroom settings.

- It is important to view our students' lives in their entirety: to see students, not just in terms of the library, but in a greater appreciation of students' full range of experiences.
- Learning about students' routines helps develop realistic views about how the library intersects with students' complicated lives.
- Creating a culture of assessment pushes the organization to focus on understanding changing customer needs and on producing value-added outcomes for customers.
- LibQUAL+ is an increasingly influential assessment tool for academic libraries.
- In the future academic libraries will become more integrated into the learning process through campus-wide collaboration in partnerships with faculty and other campus stakeholders to advance student learning outcomes.
- Academic libraries need to contribute broadly to student learning and to gain recognition for their successes.
- Colleges and universities will recognize the value of becoming student-centered learning organizations committed to continuous improvement in the quality of the education achieved by their students.
- The assessment circle is closed when information is acted upon.

NOTES

1. Edward W. Walton, "Faculty and Student Perceptions of Using E-Books in a Small Academic Institution" (paper presented at the thirteenth national conference of the Association of College and Research Libraries, Baltimore, Md., March 29–April 1, 2007), 92–99.

2. Kelly Heyboer, "New Test Finds Students' Cyber Aptitude Wanting," *Chicago Tribune*, February 18, 2007, 6.

3. Fred D. Davis, "Perceived Usefulness, Perceived Ease of Use, and User Acceptance of Information Technology," *MIS Quarterly* 13, no. 3 (1989): 319–40.

4. Susan K. Lippert and John A. Volkmar, "Cultural Effects on Technology Performance and Utilization: A Comparison of U.S. and Canadian Users," *Journal of Global Information Management* 15, no. 2 (April–June 2007): 56, 64.

5. Andy Borchers, "Wiring Watkins University: Does IT Really Matter?" *Journal of Electronic Commerce in Organizations* 2, no. 4 (October–December 2004): 30–46.

6. Susan Elwood, Chuleeporn Changchit, and Robert Cutshall, "Investigating Students' Perceptions on Laptop Initiative in Higher Education," *Campus-Wide Information Systems* 23, no. 5 (2006): 336, 345.

7. Libby V. Morris, Catherine Finnegan, and Sz-Shyan Wu, "Tracking Student Behavior, Persistence, and Achievement in Online Courses," *Internet and Higher Education* 8, no. 3 (2005): 221–31.

8. M. D. Sankey, "A Neomillennial Learning Approach: Helping Non-traditional Learners Studying at a Distance," *International Journal of Education and Development*

using *Information and Communication Technology (IJEDICT)* 2, no. 4 (November/December 2006): 82.

9. Sankey, "A Neomillennial Learning Approach," 97.

10. Brett J. L. Landry, Rodger Griffeth, and Sandra Hartman, "Measuring Student Perceptions of Blackboard Using the Technology Acceptance Model," *Decision Sciences Journal of Innovative Education* 4, no. 1 (2006): 87, 94.

11. Shery L. Shivers-Blackwell and Atira C. Charles, "Ready, Set, Go: Examining Student Readiness to Use ERP Technology," *Journal of Management Development* 24, no. 8 (2006): 802–3.

12. Ya-Ching Lee, "An Empirical Investigation into Factors Influencing the Adoption of an E-learning System," *Online Information Review* 30, no. 5 (2006): 520, 522, 524, 536–37.

13. Jong-Ae Kim, "Toward an Understanding of Web-Based Subscription Database Acceptance," *Journal of the American Society for Information Science and Technology* 57, no. 13 (2006): 1723.

14. Kim, "Toward an Understanding," 1723.

15. Diana G. Oblinger and James L. Oblinger, eds., *Educating the Net Generation* (Boulder, Colo.: EDUCAUSE, 2005), e-book at http://www.educause.edu/educatingthenetgen/ (accessed May 25, 2007).

16. Sankey, "A Neomillennial Learning Approach," 82–99.

17. Diana G. Oblinger and James L. Oblinger, "Is It Age or IT: First Steps Toward Understanding the Net Generation," in *Educating the Net Generation*, ed. Diana G. Oblinger and James L. Oblinger (Boulder, Colo.: EDUCAUSE, 2005), 2.1–2.20, e-book at http://www.educause.edu/educatingthenetgen/ (accessed May 27, 2007).

18. Judi Briden, Vicki Burns, and Ann Marshall, "Knowing Our Students: Undergraduates in Context" (paper presented at the thirteenth national conference of the Association of College and Research Libraries, Baltimore, Md., March 29–April 1, 2007), 184.

19. Briden, Burns, and Marshall, "Knowing Our Students," 186–87.

20. Briden, Burns, and Marshall, "Knowing Our Students," 188–89.

21. Amos Lakos and Shelley Phipps, "Creating a Culture of Assessment: A Catalyst for Organizational Change," *Libraries and the Academy* 4, no. 3 (2004): 359.

22. Mignon S. Adams and Jeffrey A. Beck, *User Surveys in College Libraries* (Chicago: American Library Association, 1995).

23. Xi Shi and Sarah Levy, "A Theory-guided Approach to Library Services Assessment," *College and Research Libraries* 66, no. 3 (May 2005): 266–77.

24. Association of Research Libraries, "Activities and Programs of ARL; LibQUAL+® Offers Five Events at ALA Annual Conference, Including Forum and Workshops," *ARL Communications*, E-mail News Release, May 17, 2007.

25. Peter Hernon and Robert E. Dugan, eds., *Outcomes Assessment in Higher Education: Views and Perspectives* (Westport, Conn.: Libraries Unlimited, 2004).

26. Amos Lakos, "Review of *Outcomes Assessment in Higher Education: Views and Perspectives*," *Journal of Academic Librarianship* 31, no. 4 (July 2005): 390–91.

27. Hernon and Dugan, eds., *Outcomes Assessment*, 391..

28. Cecilia L. Lopez, "A Decade of Assessing Student Learning: What We Have Learned, and What Is Next," in *Outcomes Assessment in Higher Education: Views and*

Perspectives, ed. Peter Hernon and Robert E. Dugan (Westport, Conn.: Libraries Unlimited, 2004), 29.

29. Lopez, "A Decade of Assessing," 42–46.

30. Washington State University Libraries, "Assessment Working Group," Washington State University, http://www.wsulibs.wsu.edu/general/WG/AWG.html (accessed May 24, 2007).

31. Sarah K. McCord and Mary M. Nofsinger, "Continuous Assessment at Washington State University Libraries: A Case Study," *Performance Measurement and Metrics* 3, no. 2 (2002): 68–73.

32. Elizabeth W. Carter, "Outcomes Assessment in a College Library: An Instructional Case Study," in *Outcomes Assessment in Higher Education: Views and Perspectives*, ed. Peter Hernon and Robert E. Dugan (Westport, Conn.: Libraries Unlimited, 2004), 216.

33. Peter Hernon and Robert E. Dugan, "Four Perspectives on Assessment and Evaluation," in *Outcomes Assessment in Higher Education: Views and Perspectives*, ed. Peter Hernon and Robert E. Dugan (Westport, Conn.: Libraries Unlimited, 2004), 221–22.

34. Hernon and Dugan, "Four Perspectives," 230.

35. Chris Dede, "Planning for Neomillennial Learning Styles: Implications for Investments in Technology and Faculty," in *Educating the Net Generation*, ed. Diana G. Oblinger and James L. Oblinger (Boulder, Colo.: EDUCAUSE, 2005), 15.1–15.22, http://www.educause.edu/educatingthenetgen (accessed May 25, 2007), 15.16.

36. Peter Hernon, "Preparing for the Future: A View of Institutional Effectiveness," in *Outcomes Assessment in Higher Education: Views and Perspectives*, ed. Peter Hernon and Robert E. Dugan (Westport, Conn.: Libraries Unlimited, 2004), 291–308.

37. Hernon, "Preparing for the Future," 297.

38. Peter Hernon and Robert E. Dugan, *An Action Plan for Outcomes Assessment in Your Library* (Chicago: American Library Association, 2002).

BIBLIOGRAPHY

Association of Research Libraries. *ARL Communications.* "Activities and Programs of ARL; LibQUAL+® Offers Five Events at ALA Annual Conference, Including Forum and Workshops." E-mail News Release, May 17, 2007.

Borchers, Andy. "Wiring Watkins University: Does IT Really Matter?" *Journal of Electronic Commerce in Organizations* 2, no. 4 (October–December 2004): 30–46.

Briden, Judi, Vicki Burns, and Ann Marshall. "Knowing Our Students: Undergraduates in Context." Paper presented at the thirteenth national conference of the Association of College and Research Libraries, Baltimore, Md., March 29–April 1, 2007.

Carter, Elizabeth W. "Outcomes Assessment in a College Library: An Instructional Case Study." In *Outcomes Assessment in Higher Education: Views and Perspectives*, edited by Peter Hernon and Robert E. Dugan, 197–217. Westport, Conn.: Libraries Unlimited, 2004.

Dede, Chris. "Planning for Neomillennial Learning Styles: Implications for Investments in Technology and Faculty." In *Educating the Net Generation*, edited

by Diana G. Oblinger and James L. Oblinger, 15.1–15.22. Boulder, Colo.: EDU-
CAUSE, 2005. E-book at http://www.educause.edu/educatingthenetgen (accessed
May 25, 2007).

Elwood, Susan, Chuleeporn Changchit, and Robert Cutshall. "Investigating Students' Perceptions on Laptop Initiative in Higher Education." *Campus-Wide Information Systems* 23, no. 5 (2006): 336–349.

Hernon, Peter. "Preparing for the Future: A View of Institutional Effectiveness." In
Outcomes Assessment in Higher Education: Views and Perspectives, edited by Peter
Hernon and Robert E. Dugan, 291–308. Westport, Conn.: Libraries Unlimited,
2004.

Hernon, Peter, and Robert E. Dugan. "Four Perspectives on Assessment and Evaluation." *Outcomes Assessment in Higher Education: Views and Perspectives*, edited by
Peter Hernon and Robert E. Dugan, 219–33. Westport, Conn.: Libraries Unlimited, 2004.

Hernon, Peter, and Robert E. Dugan, eds. *Outcomes Assessment in Higher Education;
Views and Perspectives*. Westport, Conn.: Libraries Unlimited, 2004.

Kim, Jong-Ae. "Toward an Understanding of Web-Based Subscription Database Acceptance." *Journal of the American Society for Information Science and Technology* 57,
no. 13 (2006): 1715–28.

Lakos, Amos. "Review of *Outcomes Assessment in Higher Education: Views and Perspectives*." *Journal of Academic Librarianship* 31, no. 4 (July 2005): 390–91.

Lakos, Amos, and Shelley Phipps. "Creating a Culture of Assessment: A Catalyst for
Organizational Change." *Libraries and the Academy* 4, no. 3 (2004): 345–61.

Landry, Brett J. L., Rodger Griffeth, and Sandra Hartman. "Measuring Student Perceptions of Blackboard Using the Technology Acceptance Model." *Decision Sciences Journal of Innovative Education* 4, no. 1 (2006): 87–99.

Lee, Ya-Ching. "An Empirical Investigation into Factors Influencing the Adoption of
an E-learning System." *Online Information Review* 30, no. 5 (2006): 517–41.

Lippert, Susan K., and John A. Volkmar. "Cultural Effects on Technology Performance and Utilization: A Comparison of U.S. and Canadian Users." *Journal of
Global Information Management* 15, no. 2 (April–June 2007): 56–90.

Lopez, Cecilia L. "A Decade of Assessing Student Learning: What We Have Learned,
and What Is Next." *Outcomes Assessment in Higher Education: Views and Perspectives*,
edited by Peter Hernon and Robert E. Dugan, 29–71. Westport, Conn.: Libraries
Unlimited, 2004.

Morris, Libby V., Catherine Finnegan, and Sz-Shyan Wu. "Tracking Student Behavior, Persistence, and Achievement in Online Courses." *Internet and Higher Education* 8, no. 3 (2005): 221–31.

Oblinger, Diana G., and James L. Oblinger, eds. *Educating the Net Generation*. Boulder, Colo.: EDUCAUSE, 2005. E-book at http://www.educause.edu/educatingth-
enetgen (accessed May 25, 2007).

Oblinger, Diana G., and James L. Oblinger. "Is It Age or IT: First Steps Toward
Understanding the Net Generation." *Educating the Net Generation*, edited by Diana G. Oblinger and James L. Oblinger, 2.1–2.20. Boulder, Colo.: EDUCAUSE,
2005. E-book at http://www.educause.edu/educatingthenetgen (accessed May
25, 2007).

Sankey, M. D. "A Neomillennial Learning Approach: Helping Non-traditional Learners Studying at a Distance." *International Journal of Education and Development Using Information and Communication Technology (IJEDICT)* 2, no. 4 (November/ December 2006): 82–99.

Shi, Xi, and Sarah Levy. "A Theory-guided Approach to Library Services Assessment." *College and Research Libraries* 66, no. 3 (May 2005): 266–77.

Shivers-Blackwell, Shery L., and Atira C. Charles. "Ready, Set, Go: Examining Student Readiness to Use ERP Technology." *Journal of Management Development* 24, no. 8 (2006): 795–805.

Walton, Edward W. "Faculty and Student Perceptions of Using E-Books in a Small Academic Institution." Paper presented at the thirteenth national conference of the Association of College and Research Libraries, Baltimore, Md., March 29–April 1, 2007.

7

Developing Power and Influence as a Library Manager

Daniel J. Julius

Aristotle State University president Reade Bookman has been discussing the importance of digital literacy and the role of the library in the twenty-first century. He has alluded to the importance of long-range planning, technology, service, and the primacy of the library in pedagogical and research endeavors. The dean of the university library, Dr. John Dewey, feels, for the first time in many years, that budget shortages may actually be made up and new programs may actually get funded. There are many needs. Dean Dewey has been lobbying for years for an increase in library funding to support new book and subscription purchases, technology updates, computers, digital learning centers, archival storage, and rare book and manuscript restoration, not to mention the need to address professional development and reclassification petitions for staff.

DEAN DEWEY IS CONFIDENT

After waiting patiently, Dewey believes (based on the president's words) it is the library's turn to reap rewards from healthy new enrollments and increased state support for the university. The provost is also enthusiastic about the library. An affable gentleman, he has always been supportive of Dewey and yet, somehow, in past years when the final budget numbers were approved, library recommendations for funding increases, not to mention new projects, went unfunded. This year, one of the new (and influential) trustees is an avid library supporter and a longtime champion of good digital citizenship. Dewey concludes that after years of relative neglect, library needs will be addressed. As the budget process unfolds,

Dewey's recommendations for new funding opportunities survive initial budget cuts. The dean is increasingly optimistic and relates, through a series of meetings with professionals and technicians working in the library, that major budgetary increases are going to materialize. Plans are revised and refined, job ads are prepared, and developmental programs are identified by Dewey's senior staff.

FINAL BUDGET PREPARATION AND APPROVAL

The budget process moves into the final phase, where the president, provost, several vice presidents, the chief auditor, a development officer, and the secretary to the board meet to approve final allocations. The provost tells Dewey he is confident, and he says the president shares these sentiments. Dean Dewey does not consult with others who will attend the allocation meeting. He takes a three-day weekend, confident of the meeting outcome.

The next week, final budgets are recommended and approved by the board. The vice president of finance distributes budget data to all senior vice presidents and deans.

DISBELIEF: BUDGET FAILURE

Unbelievably, remarkably, Dewey identifies the library allocations and quickly discerns it is simply the same amount as last year—no increase! A mistake must have been made. He calls the provost. "Yes, well, oh . . . that is what happened. . . . There were other needs, the new research center, a new student union. . . . You know I tried."

Dean Dewey is devastated. How can he face the library staff? What will it take to be successful in the budget process? Should he begin yet another career search?

A FAMILIAR REFRAIN?

Does this scenario, or variations on this theme, sound familiar? The president and the provost, Dewey's direct supervisor, were supportive. Even so, although real needs existed, they remained unfunded promises. When the dust settled, the dean ended up losing in the budget process.

The situation at Aristotle State University is not an unfamiliar saga to many library directors. Indeed, what does it take to move library priorities to the front burner? How can the dean be more influential in budget discussions? Why can't "they" see that outstanding and committed library staff, increasingly frustrated, will seek other employment? How can Dean Dewey accrue greater power and influence in order to be a more effective library manager?

POWER AND POLITICS IN ACADEMIC SETTINGS: THE ART OF INFLUENCE

This chapter will explore why Dean Dewey may not have been successful in his quest for increased budgetary support. Indeed, he has shown himself to be ineffective (exposed his lack of influence) to staff and peers, and may have damaged his relationship with the provost, as he has, at the least, caused the provost to be embarrassed at his expense. This chapter will offer general observations about power and influence in the academic decision-making environment.

To begin, what lessons can be learned from this all-too-familiar scenario involving the dean of the library at Aristotle State University?

The first lesson concerns the political nature of the university. Librarians, particularly those who ascend to higher management levels, tend to be systems-oriented and rational folks. In this regard they are, perhaps, among a select group on the "academic" side who are comfortable with institutionalized and comprehensive approaches to organizational concerns. Where some encounter difficulty, however, is in comprehending the political dynamics of the decision-making environment. Some library deans may believe budget processes are more rational and straightforward than they really are. Finally, there are those who are not comfortable engaging in the personal and professional behaviors necessary to be more influential in university environments, or who believe they are relatively powerless to effect the changes needed to be successful.

UNDERSTANDING THE DYNAMICS OF ACADEMIC DECISION MAKING

In order to understand why decisional outcomes over scarce resources are difficult, the organizational environment in which decisions are made should be understood. While consensus does not exist on this topic, the most salient characteristics of these environments are reviewed below.[1]

Decision by Committee

Because expertise, not hierarchical office, is the organizing principle, committees of experts decide many critical issues. However, in numerous instances committees provide the illusion of participation and involvement, while the real decision-making prerogatives are reserved for a small elite.

Fluid Participation

Most decision makers (often those in academic affairs) are amateurs in administration and management. Until they assumed their present position, many were primarily engaged in pursuing their professions, not in making decisions, particularly those that may lead to conflict. As a consequence, some wander in and out of the decision-making process, and power belongs to those who stay in it long enough to be effective.

An Issue Carousel

Academic issues have a way of always coming around again. Decisions are subject to pressures from outside groups, rival administrators, and students. Faculty or other influential constituencies may push the same or similar issues full circle. Decisions in academic organizations are not "made" as much as they are "pinned down" temporarily.

A "Subsidiary" Process

The longer it takes to make a decision, the greater the number of issues that get piled onto the original subject. Hoping to accomplish several things at one time, people burden simple decisions with countless subsidiary ones.

Conflict

Faculty, administrators, students, and others in the community support divergent ideas and ambiguous goals. As a consequence, conflict over goals and outcomes is common.

Interdependent Activities

Because relatively few people have formal authority over those whose support they need to be effective, it is necessary to influence executives, colleagues, supervisors, and subordinates in different departments, divisions, or schools to get things accomplished. Those who seek to be effective must learn to work through others.

Power Vacuums

Environmental vulnerability, the culture of committees, shared power, and interdependent and decentralized decision making often result in a power vacuum in academic environments. Those in leadership positions are used to working with "critics," few of whom will make tough decisions.

The image that captures the spirit of the decision-making process in an academic organization does not resemble a normal bureaucracy; does not look like the "community of peers" model associated with the medieval guild; and is not so simple as form following process, or so chaotic as to resemble a decisional garbage can. Several images are more appropriate. First, the structure of the organization is continually challenged and highly political. Second, the decision-making environment reflects competing groups. Finally, the unsettled character of the process can be captured by using the term *decision flowing* instead of decision making. Decision making has a finality to it; decision flowing sounds like a never-ending process that must be continued (and managed) in order to make outcomes really work.

UNDERSTANDING BUDGET DYNAMICS

The budget process often finds itself regressing to the status quo. It is easier to secure budgets for continuing programs and people, and difficult to secure resources for new positions and strategic initiatives. In addition, financial projections for years into the future are required. Those who develop academic programs or manage libraries, for that matter, may not know all the budget implications for new programs, services, or technological innovations. It is, in my experience, much harder to secure funds to effectuate change or start new initiatives when simply rolling over a budget is an option. Those who seek to lead in this context must convince those who control resources that reallocations reflect key (mission-related) priorities. This is not often easy, and few presidents, provosts, or deans may actually make the tough calls, particularly when the goal may be to hold onto diminishing funds while being asked to do more with less. In many large state systems, large blocks of employees are unionized, thus making it even harder to reallocate budgets, which now become subject to the vagaries of collective bargaining, state labor boards, arbitrators, and various third-party "neutrals."

In the public sector the governor, elected officials, and appointed trustees or regents are drawn into the resource debate. Chancellors and presidents may be vulnerable to politicians or rival board factions who are looking for an excuse to criticize the university or the system. This scenario often results in a decline in institutional autonomy and flexibility for academic leaders. Inevitably, the ability of vice presidents and deans to manage policy outcomes is eroded.[2] It may also be the case that institutional accounting and budgeting procedures, and individuals who oversee those processes, are more amenable to rollover scenarios. Balancing the budget can be analogous to a high-wire act, where technical expertise, long-term relationships, and an accurate prediction concerning incoming revenues are needed. Folks who are less comfortable with conflict and the political processes required to "get things done" (working through others, making "reciprocal" agreements, and the like) can be at a disadvantage.

This is not to argue that all ills befalling the academic enterprise can be traced to financial offices. Far from it. Indeed, it is often because of the political acumen, strategic thinking, and technical expertise of these individuals that universities and systems (and institutional leaders) prosper. I am suggesting, however, that in the complex decision-making environment where financial appropriations are finalized, academic provosts and deans (possibly excluding those of medicine, law, or business) may be at a disadvantage when final recommendations are forwarded to the president, regents, or trustees. Are there implications for library managers stemming from these observations? These are discussed below.

EFFECTIVE BEHAVIORS FOR BEING
MORE INFLUENTIAL IN ACADEMIC SETTINGS

A considerable body of research and excellent treatises on leadership, influence, effective administration, and the like, are available, many of which are listed in the bibliography at the end of this chapter. I would offer several observations about empowering behaviors that, to me, are essential in order to mitigate the scenario found at Aristotle State University. For the sake of expediency, I will refer to these behaviors as managing up, managing out, and managing down.

Managing Up

Simply put, those who have the opportunity (or burden, depending upon the situation) of serving as the "champions" of "your" cause must understand (and be willing and able to defend) what you are seeking. These champions (normally the provost or vice presidents) must agree to the importance of your recommendations in light of the missions of the institution and the library, know the costs associated with your causes, and, finally, be willing to articulate the consequences that may result (to students, faculty, donors, legislators, etc.) if your recommendations are not funded.

In my experience, librarians possess the information identified above but may incorrectly assume that the individuals charged with taking those messages (and recommendations) forward understand all implications and will be effective when arguments ensue. If you are not present when final decisions are being approved, you must be certain those who are present are prepared (and willing to act) with adequate background reports and summaries. Further, those who take the message forward are besieged by a multiplicity of requests. Why will yours be different? How can you, to paraphrase the words of Jerry Maguire, "help them help you"?

Two observations may be pertinent here. The first concerns a "willingness" to influence; the second, an ability to manage conflict. Effectiveness in a college or university is related to one's ability to be influential. That often means an ability to define goals, take risks by making decisions, and engage in tenacious and principled behavior. A dean who hopes to change an organization (or attain an enhanced budget) cannot simply articulate goals or a vision or objectives and sit by passively, hoping these goals or the work of others will materialize. There is no substitute for discipline, stamina, energy, focus, determination, and the art of obtaining a "commitment" from those above you in the organization. Effective leadership is also associated with managing conflict, primarily when organizational change is sought. The ability to manage conflict entails encouraging opposing groups, constituencies, or individuals to look for mutual interests, rather than focusing on respective positions. Managing conflict also demands an understanding that conflict may result from a variety of reasons: differences over facts, differences over a process to achieve particular outcomes, varying perceptions of problems at hand, or emotional differences over situational or historical factors. Defining the reasons for the conflict and finding mutually beneficial solutions, supported by a powerful constituency (or individual), are essential.

Managing Out

Being more effective requires an understanding that decision making itself can be a limited activity. When a decision is made, neither the library dean or director, nor his or her colleagues, really know with any certainty whether it is a correct or incorrect decision. Indeed, most people spend more time living with the consequences of their decisions than they do in making them. The point about decision making is this: it is important to gain support for implementing decisions and, most importantly, to know how to manage the consequences of decisions. Dean Dewey must encourage other directors or vice presidents from different units to embrace his views. Managing consequences may also mean that he must control (or at least neutralize) ever-present organizational, personal, and other competitive pressures, both internal and external, mitigating against new requests. Such pressures arise for numerous reasons: a scarcity of financial resources, tension between board members or internal leaders, requirements of accreditation bodies, state or federal dictates, workforce demands (part-time vs. full-time employment), and the desires of senates, labor unions, and the like. Most library deans, including Dewey, spend the majority of their time reacting to other people's agendas! In reality, decision-making prerogatives are constrained.

As one ascends the hierarchy in a library (or in the university), an individual has less real authority over those needed to get an idea (increased funding) or program implemented. For example, presidents often need cooperative legislators, donors, trustees, courts, or city, state, or federal officials to accomplish their agendas. Success depends on managerial savvy coupled with political persuasiveness. The most effective and influential academic administrators ask themselves if their goals are in alignment with the mission of the unit and the institution, and then select three or four priorities. Following this, they ask who else will be influential as they try to achieve their priorities. Whose cooperation and support will be needed? Whose opposition could delay or derail specific actions? What strategies or actions can be employed to gain support? Deans who "manage out" act as visionaries to colleagues and constituents who may be reluctant to embrace "their" goals, and they understand the importance of having an effective senior team. These deans realize that if senior staff are influential, their decisions are more likely to be implemented. Dean Dewey must offer internal and external groups or individuals who oppose him realistic and creative alternatives to current practices. He must find a way to turn adversaries, or simply those who are nonaligned, into allies.

Managing Down

Decisions in and of themselves do not result in action. Concrete outcomes are probable when decisional processes used to implement ideas are managed and structured, that is, committees appointed, tasks defined, priorities set, and perhaps most important, core constituencies and key individuals given a vested interest in outcomes. All leaders in the library need to engage in sustained communication with subordinates and those who are members of committees making recommendations. When constructing committees, it has been my experience that the most effective ones blend ad hoc and permanent members, given legitimacy through some kind of formal appointment. People with the most knowledge and expertise should be involved in decisions and recommendations regardless of their position or status in the library. Committee processes should be managed carefully, or endless debate may ensue. This kind of structured approach may enable those deans who seek influence to recommend solutions to the president, provost, or vice presidents that "arrive" legitimized by a "larger" group, a library constituency, if you will. It is more difficult for senior institutional leaders to ignore recommendations made pursuant to long-standing and legitimate "academic" processes.

Effective deans insist that folks in their units act in alignment with their goals and put safeguards in place to ensure, to the extent possible, that this occurs.

CONCLUSION

There is no simple antidote for Dean Dewey's problem. Indeed, the provost may be the real reason library needs remain unfunded. We can, however, offer several concluding observations that may enable Dean Dewey to marshal support for his unit. The first concerns the value of policy convergence; the second, strategic positioning; and the third, trust and integrity.

Policies and procedures establish the basis upon which people act and are evaluated, and they provide a basis whereby administrative actions are legitimized or sanctioned. Policies must support institutional values and goals. This may seem obvious, but policies are often not consistent with institutional values and goals, particularly in some smaller institutions where "control" is vested in select officers.

Here is an example where inconsistent policy encourages inefficient behavior (as well as serving to undermine the long-term goals of the dean). A policy might say that unused operational funds, rather than rolling over, return to a central pool. Library administrators who seek to safeguard funds or spend judiciously are rewarded by having remaining funds taken away. While deans may discuss effective stewardship of fiscal resources, in reality this policy encourages library managers to spend unused funds rather than losing them—often on unneeded materials, programs, consultants, and other last-minute purchases!

Effective deans ensure, not only that policies and procedures exist and are aligned, but that they reflect their own visions and priorities. Of course, policy convergence requires a broad-based review of unit rules and regulations with an eye toward the impact these policies may have on individual and institutional behavior. Conducting such reviews may entail an encounter with entrenched interests and individuals. It is important, however, to keep in mind that what people say and how policies are implemented must be consistent.

Influential deans engage in strategic positioning. They review key priorities and goals with colleagues, a senior team, or department heads. Then, as a team, they address these questions: Have short-term and long-term objectives been identified? Is the strategy to achieve objectives well defined? What will be the impact on people, functions, and policies? How will consequences be identified and assessed? How will new initiatives or programs or policies be introduced in different functional units? How will resistance within the units be handled? How will a decrease in the will to implement new ideas and programs be responded to, and what is an appropriate response? Strategic positioning is not a process that develops overnight, but over time through "managed care."

Although it seems self-evident, the most important element in any academic leader's ability to be persuasive and exercise influence is trust and integrity. To be effective, one must be seen as a person of high intellect, integrity, and probity and as an individual who can articulate a vision consistent with the values legitimized by the wider academic community. Deans are ultimately judged by their work. Reputations are solidified through excellent performance. This is one reason why it is important to have a "victory" in budget discussions. Perceptions can become reality in academic organizations. Dean Dewey must act quickly to shore up support with his senior staff. Perhaps he can convince the provost to pay a visit and have him discuss his agenda for the library. Privately, Dean Dewey may need an ironclad commitment from the provost, or other influential leader, that library needs will be addressed in the near future. Dean Dewey must reach out to colleagues and executives in other units or divisions, and he must do this in a way that doesn't make it appear as if he believes anyone is ineffectual or mean-spirited.

Finally, it might be most effective if Dean Dewey can tie the fate of the library to the agenda of the president and the success of the provost. Perhaps an enthusiastic trustee can help if that individual's support can be marshaled in an unobtrusive fashion. Enhancing one's power and influence in academic organizations does not happen quickly; neither does it happen by accident.

NOTES

1. Several notable studies and essays on higher education organizations have also discerned the political nature of human exchange processes in universities and colleges as well as in shared decision-making responsibilities. M. D. Cohen and J. G. March, *Leadership and Ambiguity: The American College President* (New York: McGraw-Hill, 1974); J. V. Baldridge, *Power and Conflict in the University* (San Francisco: Jossey-Bass, 1980); J. Pfeffer and G. R. Salancik, "Organizational Decision Making as a Political Process: The Case of a University Budget," *Administrative Science Quarterly* 19, no. 2 (1974): 131–51; R. Birnbaum, *How Colleges Work* (San Francisco: Jossey-Bass, 1988).

2. The road to university chancellor or president does not often come through financial offices. For this reason, senior leaders may be more dependent on chief financial officers or state budget directors (as opposed to provosts, deans, development officers, legislative directors) because many presidents or chancellors do not possess the expertise necessary to challenge or mediate financial recommendations. The situation in private universities is no less complex. I would argue, however, that with the exception of select wealthy institutions, institutional budgets are enrollment

and endowment driven, and those who manage revenue and revenue-enhancing functions are the most influential in decision-making processes.

BIBLIOGRAPHY

Adams, H. *The Academic Tribes*. New York: Liveright, 1976.

Altbach, Philip G., Robert O. Berdahl, and Patricia J. Gumport, eds. *American Higher Education in the Twenty-First Century*. 2nd ed. Baltimore: Johns Hopkins University Press, 2005.

Baldridge, J. V. *Power and Conflict in the University*. San Francisco: Jossey-Bass, 1980.

Baldridge, J. V. "Rules for a Machiavellian Change Agent: Transforming the Entrenched Organization. In *Managing change in educational organizations*, edited by J. V. Baldridge and T. Deal, 86–105. Berkeley, Calif.: McCutchan, 1983.

Baldridge, J. V., Davis V. Curtis, George P. Ecker, and Gary L. Riley. *Policy Making and Effective Leadership*. San Francisco: Jossey-Bass, 1978.

Bennis, W. G. *Why Leaders Can't Lead: The Unconscious Conspiracy Continues*. San Francisco: Jossey-Bass, 1989.

Bennis, W. G., and B. Nanus. *Leaders: The Strategies for Taking Charge*. New York: Harper and Row, 1985.

Bergquist, W. H. *The Four Cultures of the Academy*. San Francisco: Jossey-Bass, 1992.

Bergquist, W. H., and J. L. Armstrong. *Planning Effectively for Educational Quality: An Outcomes-Based Approach for Colleges Committed to Excellence*. San Francisco: Jossey-Bass, 1986.

Birnbaum, Robert. *How Academic Leadership Works: Understanding Success and Failure in the College Presidency*. San Francisco: Jossey-Bass, 1992.

Birnbaum, Robert. *How Colleges Work: The Cybernetics of Academic Organization and Leadership*. San Francisco: Jossey-Bass, 1988.

Bogue, E. Grady. *Leadership by Design*. San Francisco: Jossey-Bass, 1994.

Bolman, L. G., and T. E. Deal. *Reframing Organizations: Artistry, Choice, and Leadership*. San Francisco: Jossey-Bass, 1991.

Chaffee, E. E., and W. G. Tierney. *Collegiate Culture and Leadership Strategies*. Washington, D.C.: ACE / Macmillan, 1988.

Cohen, A. R., and D. L. Bradford. *Influence without Authority*. New York: Wiley, 1990.

Cohen, D. M., and J. G. March. *Leadership and Ambiguity: The American College President*. New York: McGraw-Hill, 1974.

Corson, John J. *Governance of Colleges and Universities*. New York: McGraw-Hill, 1960.

Depree, M. *Leadership Is an Art*. New York: Doubleday, 1989.

Dill, D. D. "The Nature of Administrative Behavior in Higher Education." *Administrative Science Quarterly* 20 (1984): 69–99.

Gumport, Patricia, and Barbara Sporn. "Institutional Adaptation: Demands for Management Reform and University Administration." In *Higher Education: Handbook of Theory and Practice*, edited by John C. Smart, 67–82. New York: Agathon Press, 1999.

Heifetz, R. A. *Leadership without Easy Answers*. Cambridge, Mass.: Harvard University Press, 1994.

Julius, D. "Effective Leadership in Catholic Colleges and Universities." *Current Issues in Catholic Higher Education* 24, no. 2 (Fall 2005): 53–83.

Julius, D., J. V. Baldridge, and J. Pfeffer. "A Memo from Machiavelli." *Journal of Higher Education* 70, no. 2 (March–April 1999): 113–33.

Katz, R. L. "Skills of an Effective Administrator." *Harvard Business Review*, September–October 1974, 90–102.

Kerr, Clark. *The Uses of the University*. Cambridge, Mass.: Harvard University Press, 1963.

Kezar, Adrianna. *Understanding and Facilitating Organizational Change in the 21st Century*. San Francisco: Jossey-Bass, 2001.

Kotter, J. P. *The Leadership Factor*. New York: Free Press, 1988.

Lawler, E. E., III. *The Ultimate Advantage: Creating the High-Involvement Organization*. San Francisco: Jossey-Bass, 1992.

Mortimer, K. P., and A. C. Caruso. "Governance and Reallocation in the 1990s." In *Leadership Roles of Chief Academic Officers*, edited by D. G. Brown, 34–59. New Directions for Higher Education 47. San Francisco: Jossey-Bass, 1984.

Mortimer, K. P., and T. R. McConnell. *Sharing Authority Effectively: Participation Interaction and Discretion*. San Francisco: Jossey-Bass, 1978.

Pfeffer, J. *Managing with Power: Politics and Influence in Organizations*. Boston: Harvard Business School Press, 1992.

Pfeffer, J. *New Directions for Organization Theory*. New York: Oxford University Press, 1997.

Posner, B. Z., and J. R. Kouzes. *Credibility: How Leaders Gain and Lose It, Why People Demand It*. San Francisco: Jossey-Bass, 1993.

Rosofsky, Henry. *The University: An Owner's Manual*. New York: Norton, 1990.

Walker, Donald E. *The Effective Administrator*. San Francisco: Jossey-Bass, 1979.

Whetten, D. A., and K. S. Cameron. *Developing Management Skills: Gaining Power and Influence*. New York: HarperCollins College, 1993.

8

Change Management and Risk Taking

Michael Lorenzen

SCENARIO

There was no doubt about it, Parker Brown was in trouble. He had been denying this for a few days, but as he walked to a hastily scheduled meeting with the provost, he finally admitted to himself that he was in for it. And he knew what had caused the problem too. It was those damnable periodicals!

Parker Brown reflected on how he had come to this situation. It had started innocently enough for the five-year library director of Southern Michigan University. Due to severe budget cutting by a cash-strapped state legislature, Southern Michigan University had been forced to slash hundreds of thousands of dollars from the library acquisitions budget. At the same time the funds were taken away, he was informed by his director of collection development that increases in periodical pricing would total 9.3 percent more for the next academic year. With less cash and higher prices, there would be no choice but to cancel a large number of periodical subscriptions. He knew that the faculty at Southern Michigan University would not like it, but it would have to be done.

However, as he had reflected on the situation, he began to think of another possible solution. Parker Brown had been noticing for years that the library was paying twice for many periodical subscriptions to get the content in both paper and electronic forms. Doing some number crunching, he discovered that if he canceled 60 percent of the paper periodical subscriptions that were also received electronically, he could avoid canceling any periodicals at all.

Pleased with himself for coming up with such a novel plan, he had discussed the idea with his senior staff. There were a few concerns expressed on how the move might be perceived, but other than that, they all seemed positive. Brown asked his head of public services to prepare a marketing campaign targeted at faculty and students and told his director of collection development to come up with a list of print periodicals to cancel. He sent an e-mail describing the plan to the library staff and asked the bibliographers to work with the director of collection development to help target the best periodicals for electronic access only.

Parker Brown heard nothing about the plan at all for a few weeks. His staff was working on it, and he thought all was going well. He told his provost this as well, and the provost also seemed to be happy that the library would not be losing access to any periodicals despite the steep budget cuts. And then the proverbial waste material hit the fan . . .

Brown had a meeting with Dr. Miland Jones of the psychology department. Dr. Jones was a big supporter of the library, and Brown was not surprised when he scheduled a meeting with him. However, he was stunned when Dr. Jones attacked him about the print periodical cancellation plan. He wanted to know why the psychology librarian was asking him for suggestions for canceling print journals in psychology. Jones informed Brown that this was unacceptable as he required his students to only use print resources for class assignments. He was also concerned about long-term access to the journals if they were only available electronically. Jones asked, "Can you promise me that we will have all these journals online five or ten years from now, no matter what?" Dr. Jones also offered advice on how to deal with the budget reduction. He suggested that the library lay off staff and cancel journal subscriptions that were for departments without doctoral programs.

A week later, Brown was horrified to see the periodical print reduction plan on the agenda of the faculty senate! And then, two days before the faculty senate meeting, the campus paper ran an article on the plan as well, which was critical. The headline read, "Library to Kill Journals." The article had quotes from students, faculty, and even a few of his librarians expressing concern or outrage over the whole idea. And then he had the emergency meeting placed on his schedule by the provost.

Brown had no doubt what the provost wanted to talk about. He was in for it over those periodicals, and he had yet to cancel a single print subscription! If he could not implement this plan, he would have no choice but to actually cancel access to a lot of periodicals, which would also outrage the faculty. There were no easy answers to the problem, but he expected that the provost would demand one anyway. Brown thought about a job advertisement he had seen the day before for a library dean position at a university in Ohio and decided maybe it would be a good idea to apply for it.

CHANGE MANAGEMENT AND RISK TAKING

Change is constant in the world. Very little stays as it is for long. This is true in the workplace as well. Any manager who becomes too comfortable with the way things are stands the risk of being left behind. The Bible even notes in 1 Corinthians 10:12, "Wherefore let him that thinketh he standeth take heed lest he fall." Sometimes change can come gradually, but other times it can become necessary quickly.

The world in which libraries operate has changed dramatically in the last several decades. For centuries, the basic operational structure of libraries remained unchanged. Librarians from different eras could have easily adjusted to working in libraries from different times. However, the advent of the World Wide Web and the shift of information resources to electronic format have resulted in a revolution in the ways that libraries are operated and how patrons are taught about library resources. This change in information distribution has been compared to the alteration of the publishing industry by the invention of the Gutenberg press.[1]

The world of education is constantly changing as well, which further stretches the ability of the library leader. Robert J. Starratt wrote about this when he compared being an educational leader with being a ship captain of previous centuries.[2] He wrote that these captains had to constantly scan the environment to look for signs of storms and other problems. By being alert, the captain could safely steer the ship to safety.

This is an apt analogy for library leaders today. The organization a leader is running can be seen as a ship being tossed around by turbulent waves and outside forces. How can the leader best pay attention to the changing environment and steer the institution to safety? As new technologies and political forces come to bear, this steering will often entail hard decisions about the future of the library.

Few activities create fear in the hearts of library managers like that of contemplating taking a risk or making a change. There is good reason for this reaction. However, managing change is an important job function of every library manager, and those who cannot perform this task when it is needed will fail in their role as a leader and endanger not only their jobs but perhaps their libraries as well.

This need for change will not end anytime soon. Continued changes in technology, funding formulas, laws, and so forth will dictate continued opportunities and obligations for library managers to initiate and implement change. As the consequences of these changes will be unknown, there will be an element of risk in every change endeavor. The world will change even if libraries do not, and library managers will have no choice but to make decisions about change whether the outcome is certain or not because failure to change has almost certain negative consequences.

RESISTANCE TO CHANGE

One thing that is certain for managers is that no matter how necessary a change is, there will be resistance to it in the library and perhaps in the broader community. The opposition to change may be based on good reasons, or it may be generated by those same people who oppose all change initiatives. The larger the library (and the change being proposed), the more likely that significant resistance will be encountered. This friction can sometimes be strong enough to derail a change or to make the change less effective than was intended by management.

This resistance to change is not unique to staff in libraries or even to modern times. The Roman Republic (510–27 BC) is a good example of this. The Roman people had a major problem with the concept of change. They did not like it; in fact, they were quite resistant to the idea. Tom Holland writes, "Novelty, to the Citizens of the Republic, had sinister connotations. Pragmatics as they were, they might accept innovation if it was dressed up as the will of the gods or an ancient costume, but never for its own sake."[3]

Machiavelli noted that leaders were at the greatest risk when they attempted to make changes. He wrote,

> And it ought to be remembered that there is nothing more difficult to take in hand, more perilous to conduct, or more uncertain in its success, than to take the lead in the introduction of a new order of things. Because the innovator has for enemies all those who have done well under the old conditions, and lukewarm defenders in those who may do well under the new. This coolness arises partly from fear of the opponents, who have the laws on their side, and partly from the incredulity of men, who do not readily believe in new things until they have had a long experience of them. Thus it happens that whenever those who are hostile have the opportunity to attack they do it like partisans, whilst the others defend lukewarmly, in such wise that the prince is endangered along with them.[4]

Almost five hundred years later, this tendency to resist change can be found in most organizations, including libraries. Every change a leader introduces in a library will threaten someone's position in the library. These people will instinctively fight change (actively or passively) as they feel the changes can only take away from what they already have. Conversely, those who would benefit from a change probably do not realize all the implications of the change and will be slow to rally behind the library administration in making the changes.

Inertia is another reason why change may be necessary and why it may be resisted. Often it is the library manager who is responsible for slowing down needed change. Oren Harari notes that managers often recognize that change is imperative to the organization's future yet the status quo remains.[5] One impediment to change is managers who tolerate mediocrity. Mediocrity can work its way through every part of the organization, leading to a state of inertia. The result can mean no change within the organization or instead a burst of activity that satisfies the manager's need to do something but fails to actually change anything. Harari writes,

> Breakthroughs begin when we as leaders accept the fact that good intentions are not enough. Let's also accept that simply pouring money into this quarter's reorganization or business fad will not yield the results we seek, either. The primary challenge before us is to confront the basic impediments to real change, which means ousting both cultures of mediocrity and obsessions with the quick fix. This demands a new type of leadership role, a new set of decision rules, and a new perspective on dealing with employees.[6]

Often it is the leader who is the most resistant to making changes. J. Stewart Black and Hal B. Gregersen note that organizations often fail to change for three reasons. First, they fail to see the problem. Secondly, they fail to act on the problem. Finally, they fail to follow through with a needed change. All three of these failures can be seen as additional barriers to making change. Black and Gregersen write that a failure to make needed change could be nothing less than catastrophic for an organization.[7]

What is certain is that library managers will have to manage many changes during their careers if they are to be successful. This will mean overcoming resistance in the library, in the community, and from their own desire to avoid conflict. However, resistance is likely to be present in any library when change is proposed. There are tactics and strategies that a leader can use to smooth over this resistance, but change management is always going to have an unpleasant side. Since resistance of some sort will always be present, all attempts at change management constitute some form of risk taking.

RISK TAKING

Successful managers usually have to take risks in the course of their careers, just as organizations have to take chances in order to survive. As risk taking is a form of change management, it is not surprising that risk taking also is feared by many in organizations. It may well be the risk taking itself that causes library leaders to fear change.

Robert Ramsey writes that managers must decide whether to choose and define their own risks or simply be victims of the random risks that the world presents at every turn. He argued that good managers favor being proactive by deciding for themselves when to risk, where to risk, and what to risk. Responsible risk taking implies taking carefully calculated chances and being willing to get out of the comfort zone to accomplish worthwhile goals. Since change is inevitable, the manager must decide when the right moment is to take chances.[8]

The role of the manager in deciding when to take risks is also evident in the writing of Brian Tracy. He writes that managers must take the right risks for the right reasons in pursuit of the right goals. Managers who are successful in business carefully calculate every possible risk, think about what they would do should a particular situation happen, and also have a backup plan. In addition, they minimize risk by continually questioning assumptions and asking themselves what they would do in the event of unanticipated developments. Tracy also identifies five types of risk that people face and offers advice on how to assess risk levels.[9] Tracy writes,

> So why would any sensible supervisor risk risk-taking? The easy answer is they have no choice. We all know change is the unchanging condition of business leadership. And every change involves some risk. The question for managers and supervisors is whether to choose and define their own risks or simply be a passive victim of the random risks life in the business world presents at every turn.[10]

People have different ways of approaching risk taking, according to Ralph Hyatt.[11] Tolerance for risk appears to be a stable personality aspect that impacts everyone and their daily decision making in various ways. Low risk tolerance in a person tends to go along with worrying and pessimism. People like this tend to live very carefully. People with high risk tolerance feel open and act freely. They seek change and novelty and like to live on the edge. Hyatt argued that since life is unpredictable, everyone has to take risks anyway. No one group can be classified as risk takers, but some may be better at handling risk taking than others.

Hyatt's advice is a good reminder that a manager needs to be flexible when assessing situations. As people have different preferences toward risk taking, the manager will need to keep the potential for different responses to risk taking in mind. In addition, the manager has to be aware of the environment and take risks based on the situation as well as his or her personal risk-taking style.

Most people attracted to careers in library management are not what Hyatt would describe as liking to "live on the edge." Library managers tend to gravitate more to the low side of his risk tolerance scale. However, successful library leaders move more to the center of the risk tolerance continuum. Worrying and pessimism do not lend themselves well to a successful change management philosophy any more than seeking change for the sake of novelty does. Managers should be wary of taking risks, but they also must be willing to take them when the situation calls for it.

WHAT IS NEW IS OLD

Library leaders may have to face change and risk management. One helpful technique when proposing change is to cast the new initiative as being a continuation of what is traditional in the library already. No matter what a library leader has planned, it can be made to appear to fit Ranganathan's Five Laws of Library Science.[12] Further, any change can be connected to actions and beliefs that currently exist in the library's culture. It is the job of the library leader to make any proposed change (no matter how new or novel) appear as a continuation and enhancement of past library traditions. Those leaders who can connect new changes with past practices will be the most successful.

Julius Caesar is a good example of a successful leader who was able to make significant changes by using tradition and history. One reason for this is that Caesar understood well the culture of the Roman state. It had flourished for almost five hundred years before he took power. As such, it had developed a complex set of traditions that were not to be trampled upon. As Terrence E. Deal and Kent D. Peterson note, every organization has a long past that has shaped its vision, purpose and values, rituals and ceremonies, stories and history, and artifacts and architecture.[13] This was true of the Roman Republic, and it is true for every library as well.

Holland writes, "Conservative and flexible in equal measures, the Romans kept what worked, adapted what had failed, and preserved as sacred lumber what had become redundant. The Republic was both a building site and a junkyard."[14] This is a key concept to keep in mind when contemplating the actions of Julius Caesar as he brought about the end of the Roman Republic. The government of the republic had lasted almost five hundred years (half a millennium!) despite wars, a constitutional crisis, and territorial expansion. This is twice the length of the history of the United States today. During this time, the government of the Roman Republic changed very little. Thus, the change process initiated by Caesar has to rank among the most significant of all change sequences in history.

Caesar did not visibly change the Roman Republic when he took charge. He refused the title of king. He kept the Roman Senate intact (stuffed with his supporters, of course). He also kept intact the appearance of the system of rulership of having two annual consuls. The pomp and ceremony of the Roman Republic stayed in place even after the Republic ceased to exist. Caesar successfully connected his changes to make them appear to be a continuation of the past, and in that way he made use of the existing culture of Rome to change it dramatically.

Jacob Getzels and Eton Guba write that successful organizations often have areas that die out and are then reborn.[15] This as well can be seen in Caesar's restructuring of the Roman state. Many of the institutions of the state (the Senate and the consulship, for example) died out and were re-born as the same entities with new roles. This regeneration may have been bad for democracy, but it was highly successful in the change to one-man rule for centuries to come. As such, Caesar's actions can be seen as a successful example of what Getzels and Guba were referencing.

I think Caesar's organizational changes to the Roman state are instructive to the library today. Both Deal and Peterson and Getzels and Guba have points that are important for leaders today to ponder, and studying Caesar can help them understand these points. How can a leader alter an organization and yet recognize that the culture of the organization values its past, its ceremonies, its rituals, and other expressions of what the organization has become over time? Caesar shows that change is possible and the best way to bring about change is to make the changes mesh with and seem to be a continuation of the organization's growth over time.

CHANGE MANAGEMENT MODELS

Robert Schafer writes that some managers should consider creating their own change model based on their own organizations.[16] He argued that although managers can adopt change ideas that have worked elsewhere, change is most successful when managers create their own change model through experimentation. He gives an example of this with a change model that was designed and implemented by Eagle Star Insurance. Schafer's approach is based on contingency theory, putting the impetus for designing the change model with the manager based on the manager's judgment of the organization. Schafer writes,

> For decades, CEOs have been looking for the holy grail of corporate transfor-mation. Management consultants and academics have been working overtime to supply the answer. They haven't succeeded, however, because the search is a futile one. Every organization is unique. Leaders can adopt ideas that have worked elsewhere, but they need to create their own one-of-a-kind change model through experimentation, learning, blueprint creation, and, most of all, a strong focus on results.[17]

James Huggett writes about the strategic management of organizational change in the face of organizational resistance. He argues that the key to achieving meaningful change in an organization is to align every thought, action, and behavior with the clearly defined and communicated vision. While not a cure-all for change resistance, it can help to ease many resisters through the process.[18]

In a 1967 article, H. Edward Wrapp writes about a change management approach that he calls "muddling with a purpose." He envisions the manager being patient and engaging in intense environmental scanning. When the moment is right, the leader then launches the plan with overwhelming intensity. If the leader has read the situation correctly, he or she is likely to be successful in ushering in change.[19]

THE KOTTER AND COHEN EIGHT-STEP CHANGE MODEL

This chapter started with a scenario in which a library directory got into trouble trying to initiate change in the collection development process by switching to electronic-only journals at the expense of print. While I am not going to help this unfortunate director get out of this situation, I will offer some advice on how the director could have avoided having problems in the first place. A different strategy could have perhaps avoided the controversies and drama.

I am going to base my change initiative approach on the model suggested by John Kotter and Dan Cohen in their 2002 book *The Heart of Change*. They describe an eight-step plan for change that I think could easily fit this change initiative. These steps include creating urgency, building a guiding team, getting the right vision, getting buy-in, empowering supporters, creating short-term wins, following up on victories, and making the changes stick.[20]

Creating a sense of urgency is important. Right now, many libraries have to deal with huge cuts to their budgets. This usually translates into big cuts in acquisition budgets. At the same time, publishers continue to raise prices and usually sell the same periodical to a library twice in both paper and electronic form. This model has led to a large reduction in the number of periodicals that can be purchased each year. I would make sure that this is communicated to the library staff and the patrons of a library so that the urgency to make a change in collection practices is understood.

Secondly, I would build a guiding team to help push this initiative through. Clearly, I would need to have the right department heads and bibliographers involved and supporting this measure from the beginning. In addition, I would seek out others among the library staff who wield influence. As Chester Barnard noted in 1938, oftentimes those with the most power are not on the organizational chart.[21] I would include these people when I could identify them and had reasonable assurance I could get their cooperation. Finally, the patrons of the library have to ultimately agree with the change as well. Thus, I would seek members of the university administration and faculty to also become involved in helping to guide the initiative to success.

After this, I would attempt to get the vision right. Why exactly do we need to do this and what is the right percentage of periodicals the library should receive in electronic format only? Where do I want to lead the library with this plan? As is noted in the book of Proverbs, without a vision the people will perish. If there is no coherent and attention-grabbing vision for success, it is very likely that there will be no success.

Fourth, I would communicate for buy-in. As often as possible, the guiding team and I would present the plan to library staff and library patrons and ask them to support it. This would give opportunities to answer questions, address valid concerns, identify those who oppose the change, and find new allies. Ideally, significant people will begin to agree to the change. As Black and Gregersen note, change happens a person at a time. They also postulated a 20/80 rule that if the right 20 percent of an organization's members accept a change, the other 80 percent will as well. At this stage, I would hope that the communication would get the right 20 percent to buy into the change.[22]

At the next stage, I would empower my bibliographers to act. How can they use their expertise in the subject matter to select the right journals to get only electronically? Which ones are really needed in paper? Also, I would ask them to identify those faculty most likely to support the change and get their support to make changes.

Next, I would look for short-term wins. I want to show that this plan will be successful. I would look to find bibliographers and academic departments who are eager to try the change. There are always departments in the sciences who are clamoring for more online access, so I would probably go to them to convince them to change their periodical holdings in the library to 60 percent electronic. I could then point to this as an example of progress in making the change across the entire library periodical collection. I could also cite the happiness of faculty in those departments who made the change to counter criticism to further change.

As the short-term wins started to pile up, I would shift to following up on the victories by making the change across the board to the entire library periodicals collection. As more and more wins accumulated, it would be clear that this is not an experiment or a failed collections policy but instead the new model that the library will be following in the future.

Finally, I would make the changes stick. Once the change was accomplished, it would be easy for bibliographers or faculty members to argue that certain journals should be bought on paper as well as electronically. Individually, these requests would have little impact. Collectively, though, it would undermine the completed change and could make it unravel eventually.

I believe there would be opposition to this plan both from within the organization and from outside it. Many library staff members and faculty members prefer paper holdings to electronic. Some faculty refuse to even allow their students to use electronic periodicals when writing papers. It is important to make sure that there is not an option for some staff and faculty to choose the old way while everyone else adopts the new. Making the changes stick provides resolution to the change management plan. Faculty in particular will need continued education and mentoring to help them make the transition. The continued transformation of the periodical collection will force the change whether it is accepted or not. If faculty insist on paper only in writing assignments, the students will eventually be unable to complete many of the assignments, forcing the reluctant faculty members to change their requirements.

Kurt Lewin in 1951 argued that leaders should look at a process called force field analysis when analyzing an organization.[23] One of the factors that should be looked for, he writes, are restraining forces that can prevent an organization from accomplishing a goal. In this case, what restraining forces in the force field may prevent the library from being successful? I predict the analysis would identify many of the special interests on campus (in and out of the library) who would attempt to prevent the change. Hopefully, the steps outlined in my plan based on Kotter and Cohen's process would help the library to neutralize the opposition.

CONCLUSION

Change can be hard to manage; yet change management is an integral part of being a library leader. It is hard to be successful managing a twenty-first-century library if you are unwilling to lead your library staff and the larger community down new avenues. Fortunately, many leaders have been successful in managing the change process, and there are many examples that a leader can examine for ideas. A lot of theorists have written on the topic as well, and their advice can be helpful too. The process of change management may be challenging, risky, and unpleasant, but it is also worthwhile, and the changes library leaders oversee today will hopefully make a better future for our libraries.

NOTES

1. Michael Lorenzen, "Teaching and Learning on the Web," *Academic Exchange Quarterly* 7, no. 1 (2003): 3.

2. Robert J. Starratt, *Ethical Leadership* (San Francisco: Jossey-Bass, 2004).

3. Tom Holland, *Rubicon: The Last Years of the Roman Republic* (New York: Doubleday, 2003), 4.

4. Niccolo Machiavelli, *The Prince*, 1515, http://etext.library.adelaide.edu.au/m/machiavelli/niccolo/m149p/chapter6.html (accessed January 2, 2007).

5. Oren Harari, "Why Don't Things Change?" *Management Review* 84 (1995): 30–32.

6. Harari, "Why Don't Things Change?" 32.

7. J. Stewart Black and Hal B. Gregersen, *Leading Strategic Change: Breaking Through the Brain Barrier* (New York: Prentice-Hall, 2003).

8. Robert Ramsey, "Responsible Risk Taking for Supervisors," *Supervision* 65, no. 1 (2004): 3–4.

9. Brian Tracy, "Taking Smart Risks," *National Public Accountant*, September 2003, 41–42.

10. Tracy, "Taking Smart Risks," 41.

11. Ralph Hyatt, "The Art of Healthy Risk-Taking," *USA Today*, September 1, 2001, 52–54.

12. Shiyali Ramamrita Ranganathan, *The Five Laws of Library Science* (Madras, India: Madras Library Association; London: Goldston, 1931).

13. Terrence E. Deal and Kent D. Peterson, *Shaping School Culture: The Heart of Leadership* (San Francisco: Jossey-Bass, 1999).

14. Holland, *Rubicon*, 4.

15. Jacob Getzels and Eton Guba, "Social Behavior and the Administrative Process," *School Review* 65 (1957): 423–41.

16. Robert Schafer, "Build Your Own Change Model," *Business Horizons* 47, no. 3 (2004): 33–38.

17. Schafer, "Build Your Own Change Model," 33.

18. James Huggett, "When Culture Resists Change," *Quality Progress* 32, no. 3 (1999): 35–39.

19. H. Edward Wrapp, "Good Managers Don't Make Policy Decisions," *Harvard Business Review* 45, no. 5 (1967): 91–99.

20. John Kotter and Dan Cohen, *The Heart of Change: Real-Life Stories of How People Change Their Organizations* (Boston: Harvard Business School Press, 2002).

21. Chester Barnard, *The Functions of the Executive* (Boston: Harvard University Press, 1938).

22. Black and Gregersen, *Leading Strategic Change*.

23. Kurt Lewin, *Field Theory in Social Science: Selected Theoretical Papers* (New York: Harper and Row, 1951).

9

Program Planning and Evaluation

Patrick Mahoney

SCENARIO

Western State University (WSU) is a public university with an enrollment of 8,000 undergraduate and graduate students. WSU has strong liberal arts, business, and education programs. The school's library has pioneered several electronic-based tutorial programs geared to help both new and current students increase their abilities to find, access, and use information. The library staff at the school takes pride in experimenting with technology-based tools to teach students to use information wisely. As a result of these programs, the school has built a reputation for developing information literacy (IL) services for both students and faculty.

Recently, the school began to offer its graduate programs in business and public administration to distance learning students. In order to meet the distance learning students' specific needs, the school examined its mix of electronic resources and the technology needed to deliver these resources to these students. Based on the early success of these initial programs, WSU is considering expanding its distance learning programs to include education degrees.

WSU librarians typically teach one-shot IL sessions to individual classes, typically arranged by faculty around an assignment or research topic. The librarians find it difficult to cover all aspects of the research process and all the information sources used to provide information. Many of the librarians feel that, because of the single opportunity to instruct students on IL, there is little ability to communicate additional information to students. This is especially challenging in working with distance learning students. As a result, on-campus students are highly encouraged to visit the subject librarians to further discuss their projects.

Raymond Kingston is the head of instructional technology with the university's library. He has held that position for over five years and has been the primary leader in the library's development of electronic resources. Up to now, his practice has been to develop and implement new informational instructional technologies and services with minimal communication with anyone outside the library. Essentially, he and other librarians introduce new forms of instructional tools that they have identified through reading about their applications and uses in traditional library literature and attending library conferences. There they exchange ideas with fellow librarians on what technologies and programs seem to work best with students.

Linda Phelps is one of the reference librarians at WSU, a position she has held since her graduation from library school two years ago. She specializes in working with the education students and faculty to develop reference and literacy programs. She has a love for using new forms of technology to reach out to her students and jumps at the chance to see how effective these new tools might be in teaching information literacy skills to them. Together Linda and Raymond have worked hard to examine new technologies to improve IL services for WSU's students.

Research, Planning, and Implementation

One year ago Raymond decided to implement blogs as an additional tool for IL instruction. He has been personally active in blogging with library organizations and sites outside the library realm. Because of his love of technology and his initial belief that all young people use blogs as a form of communication, he is interested in exploring the value of blogs for IL instruction at WSU.

Raymond conducted preliminary research on the use of blogs within academic libraries. A Google search provided many hits; however, the information was broad and difficult to synthesize. He also conducted searches in the professional literature only to find that the use of blogs appeared primarily in the areas of reference, library news and discussion, outreach, marketing, and internal communication; very little was reported on the successful implementation of blogs in IL or even on the use of blogs in an IL role.

Still, Raymond was excited about blogs. Given the growing popularity of blogs with young people as a means of interaction and communication, Raymond decided to use them in an IL instruction role. He recruited Linda to codevelop a plan for the inclusion of blogs into the library's IL instructional toolkit.

Two goals were established for the use of blogs in an IL instruction role. The first goal was to encourage communication and improve upon communication channels between librarians and traditional and distance learning students. The second goal was to encourage students to engage in open dialogue on research issues, thus encouraging collaborative learning.

During the spring and fall semesters of 2004, Raymond used Google's Blogger to create a blog for each of ten classes for which he and Linda provided face-to-face IL instruction. A blog was also created for one distance education class.

Raymond and Linda marketed their new IL service through many channels. In the spring semester, students were introduced to blogs during face-to-face IL sessions. Blog information was printed on traditional handout material and related contact material. Distance education students and faculty were alerted to blogs through e-mail. Also, all the blogs were linked to subject guides on the library's website.

The fall semester brought changes to the librarians' marketing plan. In addition to the above, flyers consisting of handouts of the blog's first pages were distributed during face-to-face sessions. These handouts stated the purpose of the blogs, instructions for students to leave comments, and librarian contact information.

Raymond and Linda utilized an open-source hit counter on some of the blogs to record the number of visits to each blog. The counters were not, however, configured to distinguish between students visiting the sites to blog and Raymond making updates.

Raymond and Linda posted information to the blogs periodically during both semesters. Research tips, website evaluations, electronic information resources not covered during typical IL sessions, new services available to faculty and students, and information about remote access were among the topics presented.

Evaluation and Solutions

To gauge the effectiveness and usage of the blogs, Linda developed a survey. The survey's URL was posted with each blog. Raymond and Linda asked faculty to encourage their students taking classes where blogs were available to take the surveys.

The number of survey responses was very low. Only 15.3 percent, or 31 of the 202 targeted students, responded to the spring survey. Of these, only 5 of the 31 students stated that they had blogged, or even read other blog postings. Furthermore, 71 percent of the respondents reported that they never checked their class's research blogs, and none of the remaining 29 percent used the blog's comments feature.

Next, 46 percent of those who responded to the survey felt the blogs were not very helpful. Many respondents stated that they never used the blogs, did not know anything about the availability of the blogs, or did not know anything about blogs in general. Interestingly, almost 40 percent of the respondents stated the need for increased marketing of the blogs.

Only 2 out of 105 targeted students responded to the fall survey. Both students were part of a distance education class, with one an admitted recreational blogger. That student reported checking the blog once without posting a comment and felt the blog was not very helpful. The other respondent stated that he or she did not check the blogs for new postings unless directed to do so.

Nonetheless, the blogs received some positive comments. The two fall respondents, along with some of the spring respondents, felt the blogs had some useful information posted by Raymond and Linda, and the respondents liked the convenience of accessing this information online.

In order to gauge the opinions of fellow instruction librarians on the use of blogs, Linda developed a survey that was distributed through a national library association's website. While the survey did not directly relate to WSU's IL blogging efforts, Linda and Raymond wished to see if blogs were used and, if so, whether they were well received by those librarians and their institutions.

Ninety people responded to that survey, of whom seventy worked at four-year academic institutions. All reported at least some familiarity with blogs. Thirteen of the respondents used blogs to communicate with their own students. Blog topics covered many areas: literature research, Internet access for both traditional and distance learning students, and course-specific information. Only eight respondents felt improvements were necessary, with the main area of concern being the marketing of blogs. Another question asked whether blogs had any use in IL. Of the thirty-five who replied to the question, fourteen felt blogs were a valuable tool. Several respondents felt that the success of blogs for IL was highly dependent on the support of faculty. Five respondents stated that blogs served the same function as discussion and bulletin boards characteristic of many courseware products, thus making blogs redundant.

ANALYSIS

Based on the two surveys presented to WSU students and the feedback provided by the national survey, Raymond and Linda felt their efforts in using blogs for IL purposes did not meet expectations. The goal of motivating students to engage in discussion on learning additional research skills was not met as no student posted a comment on a blog. The other goal, to continue to teach IL skills to both traditional and distance learning students, also was not fully realized as few students took the time to explore the IL blogs.

Raymond and Linda's effort to explore new avenues and technologies to reach out to students at WSU was commendable. Several issues should have been addressed during the initial information-gathering stage of their IL blog idea and during the planning stage prior to implementing the service. One of those issues is the need to make better use of existing research in the development and formulation of a plan. The solutions discussed below are applicable to any library that desires to offer similar programming services to enhance information literacy efforts for their students. Specifically, Raymond and Linda needed to improve their efforts in these areas:

- Understanding the cultural and societal implications of technology
- Collaboration with faculty and other key players in the use of blogs
- Improvements in marketing efforts
- Implementing an IL blog pre-survey and post-survey

Understanding the Cultural and Societal Implications of Technology

Libraries have a long tradition of implementing technology that enhances the access and retrieval of information. College and university libraries have also implemented technology to improve their IL services to their students, especially those who are taking classes away from brick-and-mortar classrooms. Librarians involved with IL activities for distance learning students must use technology to reach those students since traditional face-to-face methods to reach them are not a viable option.

Not all technologies, however, may be suitable for specific library services. Even though segments of society embrace new technologies to recreate or communicate, that does not mean the technologies are excellent candidates for specific library services, including information literacy instruction. The use of blogs serves as an example. Raymond loves to blog, and his desire to use this service may have clouded his judgment, leading him to recruit Linda and implement this web-based communication service for IL without the appropriate planning.

In order to assess the applicability of blogs as an IL tool, Raymond and Linda needed to understand the cultural and societal characteristics of those environments that promote the use of blogs. Many of these environments revolve around virtual communities. Virtual communities are online environments that usually center on a limited subject area or related subject areas. People use virtual communities because they can share ideas and information with other virtual members with similar interests. Blogging on these virtual communities provides participants a feeling of belonging and membership; virtual communities provide members a sense of community.[1]

Most of the IL blogs were administered for classes where the librarians had face-to-face interactions with the students. Traditional brick-and-mortar environments where people see each other regularly are not conducive to blogging. Most environments that feature blogs as an integral vehicle for members to communicate tend to be virtual communities with members widely dispersed from each other.[2] Traditional students taking classes together at set times in a physical environment may not utilize blogs as much as distance learning students do. Distance learning students would be much more likely to use technological means to communicate and learn as they essentially have no other ways to accomplish these tasks.

Raymond and Linda needed to explore the characteristics of virtual communities and how blogging enhances the users' experiences in these communities. The old saying, "If you build it, they will come," may apply in some circles, but not necessarily for library services.[3] Raymond's love for this medium of electronic communication may not have been enough justification to initiate the use of blogs for IL instruction without additional thought as to the relationship of blogging and virtual communities.

Collaboration

The need for librarians to collaborate with faculty to advance teaching and learning is significant and has been a challenge for the profession since library instruction became formalized. Collaboration with faculty can be a difficult process; many faculty, while appreciative of the librarians' efforts to increase literacy with students, often do not consider their efforts critical in course planning and teaching.[4]

Still, Raymond and Linda did little to foster collaboration with WSU faculty and students during the planning and design stages of the IL blog service. Other than to provide the IL blogs for each of the ten courses, little if any interaction took place between the two librarians and any other faculty. Reaching out to faculty is crucial to the success of any library service. In addition to expert insight into their students' needs, faculty offer a direct link to the students themselves.[5] Faculty are also the gatekeepers for inclusion of library programs and services into their curricula.

Raymond and Linda needed to identify those faculty most likely to utilize technology and additional communication services such as blogs. These and other champions needed to be identified early during the planning stages of the IL blog project.[6] Collaboration with faculty and other professionals can also lead to valuable networks consisting of other potential candidates for inclusion in the planning process.[7] Additional collaborative efforts with not only faculty but other people at WSU involved with educational and informational services to students should have been undertaken.

Marketing

Raymond and Linda marketed the blogs using several techniques. Students were notified using a variety of tools including face-to-face meetings, some printed material, subject guides, and e-mail. Still, both Raymond and Linda felt these marketing efforts had little impact on the students. Both librarians were afraid that any additional marketing efforts would have resulted in an increased use of blogs at the expense of other communication tools such as telephone, e-mail, personal visits, and so forth. The designing, planning, and implementation of an IL blog service implied the desire for success of the service. In order to reach the service's full potential, all marketing techniques should have been fully exploited.

An important marketing ingredient that should have been included in the original marketing mix is the faculty at WSU. If collaboration is an important element in the design and implementation of a new blog service, then the inclusion of the faculty in the marketing plan would have been a necessity. Raymond and Linda should have informed the faculty as to what benefits they could enjoy by recommending the blogs to their students. By equating the blogs to increased student productivity, and better projects and assignments, faculty may have taken the time to more aggressively promote the blogs to their students.[8]

Raymond and Linda conducted an isolated marketing campaign in their effort to promote their IL blog program that produced less than meaningful results. Marketing services lend themselves to building relationships over time. Relationship marketing encourages consistent educational communication to customers, or the faculty in this case, of new products or services.[9] Constant communication over time is the key component in relationship marketing. In order for Raymond and Linda to maximize their marketing efforts for future IL services, they will need to have ongoing and consistent dialogue with the faculty of WSU. Relationship marketing is not a one-time promotional gimmick; rather, it requires effort and time to reap its full benefits.

By not including faculty in the marketing mix, the two librarians exercised ineffective marketing. Effective marketing techniques tend to segment a targeted audience into smaller and manageable units. By concentrating on the smaller units, more information can be obtained to create better marketing programs.[10] In this case, Raymond and Linda could have exercised effective marketing by examining each possible segment or unit of their target group. As an example, distance learning faculty at WSU could have been treated as a single marketable unit. A distinct marketing program geared to their needs, wants, and desires could have been crafted.

Relationship and effective marketing take time and effort to properly craft; however, the rewards are much greater than creating plans for just one segment. In this case, only the students were targeted for marketing efforts by the librarians.

Pre-Surveys and Post-Surveys

Prior to Raymond and Linda's decision to implement a large-scale IL instruction service, they could have examined a smaller segment of the program. This way both librarians could have tweaked the service based on the test sample. A cooperative faculty member could have been contacted to see if he or she might be willing to use IL blogs in one course during a semester. At the end of the course, both librarians and the faculty member could dissect the survey results to see what areas of improvement could be made before rolling out a finished product.

Surveys were used to assess student use and activity of the IL blogs after each of the two semesters. A pre-survey could have been administered as a useful tool to determine if the blogs actually did provide useful information to students even if they stated afterward that they did not post questions or comments to the blogs. Only 15 percent of the students stated they checked their IL blogs. Pre-surveys and post-surveys are useful for immediate outcomes of instructional sessions.[11] If properly constructed, a pre-survey and a post-survey could have identified the effectiveness of the blogs for those who actually read them. In this case, both surveys would have to assess desired student learning outcomes. Once these outcomes could be identified and assessed using both surveys, Raymond and Linda could have extracted more meaningful information than was available to them with only a post-survey and with no measurable student learning outcomes.

A pre-survey and a post-survey on the effectiveness of blogs would have been excellent candidates for inclusion with the librarians' IL tool, as long as the nature of the surveys would be to gauge the relationship the blogs had in the students' process of acquiring knowledge (learning outcomes).[12]

CONCLUSION

Numerous factors contribute to successful online programs and services: research, planning, faculty development, technical support, student services, curricular design, technologies, and course design.[13] Of these, Raymond and Linda needed improvement in collaborative efforts with faculty, understanding of technologies and their environments, and research efforts. And they needed to at least implement a pre-survey as a means of gauging any change in learning outcomes caused by the presence of the blogs. Finally, Raymond and Linda might want to reexamine the role IL blogs play for WSU's distance learning students. The environment those students participate in will be more conducive to integrating blogs into WSU's IL tool kit.

Librarians are eager to implement new technologies to enhance their current services and to improve students' information literacy. Introducing new technologies with little regard to assessing student outcomes, initiating marketing plans, and developing long-term relationships through collaboration will only undermine the effectiveness these technologies can offer. By following these suggestions, better technology-based services can be implemented with minimal fuss and increased student participation.

NOTES

1. Anita Blanchard, "Blogs as Virtual Communities: Identifying a Sense of Community in the Julie/Julia Project," *Into the Blogosphere*, http://blog.lib.umn.edu/blogosphere/blogs_as_virtual.html (accessed February 7, 2007).

2. "Learning Spaces: Social Networks," *High Tech Learning*, http://www.eduscapes.com/hightech/spaces/social/index.htm (accessed February 10, 2007).

3. Jill S. Markgraff, "Collaboration Between Distance Education Faculty and the Library: One Size Does Not Fit All," in *Distance Learning Library Services: The Tenth Off-Campus Library Services Conference*, ed. Patrick B. Mahoney, 451–64 (Binghamton, N.Y.: Haworth Information Press, 2002).

4. Joyce Lindstrom and Diana D. Shonrock, "Faculty-Librarian Collaboration to Achieve Integration of Information Literacy," *Reference & User Services Quarterly* 46, no. 1 (Fall 2006): 19.

5. Markgraff, "Distance Education Faculty and the Library."

6. Joanna M. Burkhardt, Mary C. MacDonald, and Andree J. Rathemacher, *Creating a Comprehensive Information Literacy Plan* (New York: Neal-Schuman, 2005), 4.

7. Markgraff, "Distance Education Faculty and the Library."

8. Burkhardt, MacDonald, and Rathemacher, *Comprehensive Information Literacy Plan*, 103.

9. Irene Owens, "Marketing in Library and Information Science: A Selected Review of Related Literature," in *Strategic Marketing in Library and Information Science*, ed. Irene Owens, 5–31 (Binghamton, N.Y.: Haworth Information Press, 2002).

10. Owens, "Marketing in Library and Information Science."

11. Burkhardt, MacDonald, and Rathemacher, *Comprehensive Information Literacy Plan*, 96.

12. Sheila Young and Julia C. Blixrud, "Research Library Involvement in Learning Outcomes Assessment Programs," *ARL* no. 230/231 (October/December, 2003), 1–4, http://firstsearch.oclc.org/images/WSPL/wsppdf1/HTML/07028/WDUP8/9SO.HTM (accessed February 12, 2007).

13. Elizabeth A. Buchanan, "Institutional Challenges in Web-Based Programs: Student Challenges and Institutional Responses," in *The Eleventh Off-Campus Library Services Conference Proceedings*, ed. Patrick B. Mahoney, 65–74 (Binghamton, N.Y.: Haworth Information Press, 2005).

BIBLIOGRAPHY

Blanchard, Anita. "Blogs as Virtual Communities: Identifying a Sense of Community in the Julie/Julia Project." *Into the Blogosphere.* http://blog.lib.umn.edu/blogosphere/blogs_as_virtual.html (accessed February 7, 2007).

Buchanan, Elizabeth A. "Institutional Challenges in Web-Based Programs: Student Challenges and Institutional Responses." In *The Eleventh Off-Campus Library Services Conference Proceedings,* edited by Patrick B. Mahoney, 65–74. Binghamton, N.Y.: Haworth Information Press, 2005.

Burkhardt, Joanna M., Mary C. MacDonald, and Andree J. Rathemacher. *Creating a Comprehensive Information Literacy Plan.* New York: Neal-Schuman, 2005.

Harmon, Glynn. "The Importance of Marketing in the Library and Information Science Curriculum." In *Strategic Marketing in Library and Information Science,* edited by Irene Owens, 61–79. Binghamton, N.Y.: Haworth Information Press, 2002.

"Learning Spaces: Social Networks." *High Tech Learning.* http://www.eduscapes.com/hightech/spaces/social/index.htm (accessed February 10, 2007).

Lindstrom, Joyce, and Diana D. Shonrock. "Faculty-Librarian Collaboration to Achieve Integration of Information Literacy." *Reference & User Services Quarterly* 46, no. 1 (Fall 2006): 18–23.

Markgraff, Jill S. "Collaboration Between Distance Education Faculty and the Library: One Size Does Not Fit All." In *Distance Learning Library Services: The Tenth Off-Campus Library Services Conference,* edited by Patrick B. Mahoney, 451–64. Binghamton, N.Y.: Haworth Information Press, 2002.

Owens, Irene B. "Marketing in Library and Information Science: A Selected Review of Related Literature." In *Strategic Marketing in Library and Information Science,* edited by Irene Owens, 5–31. Binghamton, N.Y.: Haworth Information Press, 2002.

Royse, David, Bruce A. Thyer, Deborah K. Padgett, and T. K. Logan. *Program Evaluation: An Introduction.* 3rd ed. Belmont, Calif.: Thomson Learning, 2001.

Young, Sheila, and Julia C. Blixrud. "Research Library Involvement in Learning Outcomes Assessment Programs." *ARL* no. 230/231 (October/December 2003): 14–17. http://firstsearch.oclc.org/images/WSPL/wsppdf1/HTML/07028/WDUP8/9SO.HTM (accessed February 12, 2007).

10

Moving into Leadership

Kathleen Walsh

Why worry about leadership? Because it's scary out there! Librarianship is in a desperate (existential?) struggle to find its soul and reinvent itself for the twenty-first century. Good management can carry organizations through periods of stasis and stability. But change demands leadership to take us from where we are now to where we need to be (or want to be but don't yet know it).[1] Consider the following:

- Digital technology changes everything.[2]
- Our nation is facing a demographic revolution.
- Institutions of higher education are facing bottom-line competitive pressures.
- Universities and their libraries are facing reduced funding from all sources.
- The pace is turbulent, disruptive, transformative—and accelerating.
- You'll be "leading from the middle," as Joan Gallos describes it:[3] you'll have more responsibility than authority, and you'll be answerable to constituents above and below you in the hierarchy, as well as to your "customers." This "dean's squeeze" (Gallos's term) makes it tough to balance competing interests.
- Don't underestimate the power of the status quo.[4] Academics and academic institutions have a mighty and historic resistance to change.
- Let's be honest, if a bit politically incorrect—the "librarian personality" often comes with a streak of congenital shyness. Leadership will require you to separate your *self* from your *role*, and to be conscious of the difference. (You'll actually find this very liberating!)

- You probably have little or no formal training in management, let alone leadership. And it may take a while to realize that there's a 180-degree turn involved in moving from management to leadership—and that the behaviors that made you a great manager can work against you as a leader.

What follows are the lessons that textbooks and similar resources don't teach very effectively and that have made the difference for me in my own ability to succeed—that is, to get things right more often than I get them wrong. These lessons have been hard-earned, and they might be helpful for others following similar paths.

- As an academic library director or dean, you'll be seeing a lot of PowerPoint presentations. Your institution's high-level planners and administrators use them all the time. You'll probably be expected to use them too.
- So it seemed sensible to use bulleted lists, a key feature of most PowerPoint presentations, in this chapter. (The medium is part of the message.)
- In a real presentation, it's a bad idea to use a lot of words (see Mistake No. 9 below), *pace* Edward Tufte.[5]

Consider the following 180-degree turn from manager to leader:[6]

Management Focus

- Doing things right
- Urgency
- Speed
- Bottom line
- Efficiency
- Methods
- Practices
- In the system
- Climbing the ladder fast

Leadership Focus

- Doing the right things
- Importance
- Direction
- Top line

EFFECTIVENESS

Stephen Covey uses the preceding framework as shorthand to delineate the essential differences between management and leadership. In every way, leadership requires broader perspective, broader knowledge, and broader goals. Covey also identifies four imperatives for great leaders:[7]

- Inspire trust among direct reports, superiors, and peers.
- Align systems and work processes so they facilitate rather than hinder achievement.
- Clarify purposes by articulating why goals are established and how individual work contributes to those goals.
- Unleash the unique talents and contributions of people on their teams.

We can identify leadership competencies at three levels (they're scalable and simultaneous).[8]

Leading at the Top

- Create vision and set direction.
- Focus on "what might be."
- Think strategically, have insight, and see long-term.

Leading at All Levels

- Inspire, influence, and persuade others to follow.
- Act decisively.
- Create an environment that allows and cultivates the achievement of the vision or mission and desired outcomes.
- Lead strategically, effectively, and by best practices.
- Build or develop a competent, diverse, and empowered organization (this includes developing future leaders).
- Model the way.
- Possess self-knowledge, accept responsibility, and exhibit emotional maturity.

Leading from Within

- Translate vision, mission, and strategy into action.
- Align systems, structures, and processes with strategy.
- Maintain customer focus.
- Possess the ability to follow as well as lead.

MY OWN TOP TEN DON'TS

As you move into leadership, never, ever, ever underestimate the following:

1. The importance of your own personal credibility and passion
2. The power of a compelling vision
3. The necessity of politics and of understanding organizational dynamics
4. The differences between management and leadership, and between tactics and strategy
5. The critical importance of trend spotting as a way of life—combined with an awareness of the many environments in which the library operates
6. The reality that not everyone loves libraries or sees a need for librarians or their work
7. The strength that's gained by delegating responsibility and authority
8. How much you can accomplish if you don't care who gets the credit[9]
9. The beauty of brevity
10. The imperative to look for opportunities, take risks, and innovate

KAREN'S FIRST LEADERSHIP EXPERIENCE, OR HOW NOT TO LEAD

Karen Weeks strained to feel comfortable at the informal reception that Acme University's board of trustees was hosting for the university's academic administrators. Until three weeks ago the access services department head, Karen had just been appointed interim dean of the Acme library, succeeding a predecessor who had resigned abruptly; and this was her first direct contact with the people who were ultimately responsible for Acme University's well-being. Although intensely self-conscious, Karen appreciated that this kind of opportunity came rarely, and she meant to make the most of it.

Karen made nervous small talk with each board member to whom Acme University's provost (Karen's new boss) introduced her. After friendly welcomes from several people, Karen found herself with board member Paul Andre. Paul was CEO of Andre & Co.—yes, *that* Andre & Co.—and he wasn't smiling. Karen had heard about him. She was aware of Andre & Co.'s reputation as premier business consultants, and she'd been warned that Paul didn't suffer fools gladly. She introduced herself and thanked him for the chance to meet board members personally.

Paul Andre looked directly into Karen's face, unblinking. His response startled her. "Nice to meet you. But you know, I have to say I wonder sometimes about the library. It seems to me the university wastes a lot of money on library stuff that doesn't get used and people who sit around all day with not much to do." He munched a celery stick and waited for her answer.

Karen stammered, "Well, you know, you can't always see the immediate effects. But, um, well, libraries have always been the heart of every great university and that certainly isn't going to change."

No response, though Paul's gaze stayed fixed on her. He remained silent as, fumbling, she tossed more words into the void. But finally he spoke, slowly and deliberately. "I'm founder and CEO of Andre and Company. You've heard of us? Good. I've got a Wharton MBA and a Harvard law degree. And I have never spoken to a librarian. Never. In my life. I'm not sure I've set foot in a library since I was ten years old." Paul paused, and then challenged her directly: "Make me care."

Paul waited for Karen's answer. She didn't have one.

Paul moved away, but he had one more comment. "This university is in crisis, understand? Crisis. You're not telling me how your library can help."

As it happened, Karen had been invited to do a short presentation at the next quarterly board meeting, two weeks later. The board members were interested in what plans she might have for transforming the Acme library for the twenty-first century and the new generations of students Acme would be admitting. Karen worked up a fifteen-minute PowerPoint presentation that described in detail how the library would expand its book collections and its circulation and interlibrary loan operations. She would also be asking for significant remodeling and expansion of library space. She'd be overseeing all these changes personally, to ensure that things would go smoothly. The entire library faculty and staff had actually contributed to this plan, which Karen had inherited from her predecessor; but since the board had asked for her ideas, Karen thought it best to present it as her own.

The appointed evening came, the board convened, and Karen found herself launching into the PowerPoint, following a tight script to be sure she could keep her thoughts together. As she talked on, Karen never noticed the stifled yawns and fidgets overtaking her listeners.

When Karen finished, to polite applause, the chair invited questions. There was only one, and it came from Paul Andre. "I appreciate your work on this, but I can't see how it's helpful to Acme University. I mean, the library you're describing is old. It's out of touch. It seems like more of a disservice to our faculty and students than a service. The faculty aren't going to be able to keep up in their research fields, and I can't understand how you're going to reach this generation of students. Have you thought of any alternatives?"

This wasn't what Karen had expected.

Face flushing, she answered, "Well, this plan builds on our tradition of service and every year on the graduating student survey the students rank our library as the best service in their Acme experience and when they come into the library they like it and—"

Paul interrupted her torrent of words. "OK, so students like you. Do they learn anything from you?"

"Well, of course they do. You know—they learn how to write their research papers and they learn how to use the computers and search the databases and—"

He cut her off again. "How do you know? Can you demonstrate that they're learning anything that they can take away and use in their lives?"

Dead silence followed. Karen didn't have an answer. Was her library in fact accomplishing its academic mission? She couldn't say.

Another question from Paul Andre. "How much did you spend on books last year?"

"Uh—about a hundred fifty thousand. I think we bought about three thousand books."

"Mm-hm. How many of those books actually got checked out of the library?"

"Um—uh—well, I don't know exactly how many of them got checked out—"

"How many books from whatever year got checked out during the last twelve months?"

"Well, we did a circulation of about—our total circulation was around—um, I think maybe about four thousand books."

"Four thousand books. And we have eight thousand students. Are you telling me each student at Acme checked out one half of one book this past year? And as I understand it, we're also paying for interlibrary loan through a consortium. So—how many of the books that did circulate actually went to our own students and faculty?"

Karen drew a blank.

Paul persisted. "In other words, how much of that hundred fifty thousand dollars, plus the consortium costs—how many of those dollars are directly supporting Acme students' learning and Acme faculty research?"

After a long pause, Karen almost whispered, "I'll find the numbers and get back to you." She thanked the board for their time, gathered up her papers, and left.

Two weeks later, the following year's budget was announced. Karen discovered to her horror that the library's budget had been cut by 20 percent overall, which incorporated a 50 percent cut to the book budget. And the provost was requesting an 8 a.m. meeting with Karen the following day.

WHAT WENT WRONG?

Mistake No. 1

Karen undermined her own credibility and didn't communicate passion. Instead, she communicated fear and confusion. She did not convince her audience that she personally believed, or even fully understood, what she was saying. She wasn't prepared with facts and figures. And she didn't seem to understand her library's significance within the larger context of Acme University's operations. Never, ever, ever . . .

- forget that your own credibility is the coin of the realm and your greatest strength. The people you're working with must know that you're telling the truth as you see it, and that you personally believe in the library's importance.
- blur the difference between your *self* and your *role* (or roles). You've moved from department manager to designated spokesperson for the entire library, and designated maker of unpleasant decisions. This role has its own responsibilities that are separate and apart from your personal identity. It can be much, much easier to speak out and to make hard decisions if you can keep that in mind. It's not about *you*—it's about "the library dean."
- be afraid to advocate for your library. *But*—understand and appreciate that you're also an officer of your university or college. There will be times when those larger interests will override the library's more immediate interests. Know when to advocate for your institution versus for your library per se.

Mistake No. 2

Karen had no vision. She didn't paint a compelling picture for her listeners to grasp. Instead, she clung to old bromides and a musty, fusty image of a pile of books inside a pile of bricks. The Acme University board members were looking for something exciting and in tune with the times. Karen didn't lead them there. Never, ever, ever . . .

- forget you're responsible for giving other people hooks to hang ideas on—mental pictures that will help them understand your ideas so they can support and develop them.
- get caught up in looking inward and backward. You can't move forward if you're busy doing that. To move your library into the future, you'll need to be looking outward and forward.

- think "vision" is a more complicated concept than it actually is. What does your mind's eye see when you imagine a future for your library? The details may be fuzzy, but you can probably define the general outline pretty clearly. If not, keep thinking about it until you can see it for yourself and convey it to other people. Use your imagination! And make sure that whatever you're imagining is exciting, compelling, and of real value.

Mistake No. 3

Karen didn't comprehend the power and the necessity of politics. Instead, she treated her interactions with the board as performances, rather than opportunities to build alliances and relationships. She seemed to react to Paul Andre only as an enemy, and failed to understand that his "agenda" might in fact represent fully legitimate concerns and interests. Never, ever, ever . . .

- forget that your role is to influence how other people think and behave, on your library's behalf. "Make me care"—yep, that's an essential leadership role and responsibility.
- underestimate the imperative to build alliances and partnerships that mutually benefit both your library's and your partners' constituents. That's the essence of politics, and there's nothing evil about it.
- fail to understand that *everyone* has an agenda—usually more than one. You do too. Your agenda reflects your legitimate interests. So do other people's agendas, at least most of the time. And there's nothing evil about that either. (Hint: It's hugely helpful to understand the differences between interests and positions, and to master the art of "getting to yes"[10] through negotiation. And it's completely possible to "say no and still get to yes."[11])

Mistake No. 4

Karen didn't separate tactics from strategy, or effective management from effective leadership. She kept on functioning the way a manager would: by focusing on intricate detail and making sure that the library would get those details right. She wasn't looking at the much larger, strategic issues:

- What would be the library's mission, vision, and values going forward?
- What would be its unique and enduring contribution to the lives of Acme students and faculty?
- How would the library contribute to Acme University's overall success as an educational institution?

- How would the library fulfill its academic mission as well as possible?
- How would she know? How would the library's effectiveness be measured?

Never, ever, ever . . .

- forget that the characteristics and behaviors that made you a great manager can incapacitate you as a leader.
- get so hung up in details that you lose sight of the biggest picture— library-wide, institution-wide, profession-wide.
- forget your responsibility to see that your library *does the right thing*— rather than just doing things right.

Mistake No. 5

Karen didn't seem to be aware of trends or to comprehend that her library was operating in multiple and changing environments. Her conversation and her presentation suggested she was unaware of, or ignoring, the technological and social revolutions going on all around her—not to mention being utterly unaware of the board's interests, or even those of students and faculty.

Never, ever, ever . . . lose sight of the vital importance of spotting trends:

- Social transformations wrought by the Internet
- Demographic changes
- Business environments for institutions of higher education
- The evolving library landscape
- Changes in scholarship and scholarly communication
- Any other developments in the wider world that would likely affect students, faculty, or library strategy or operations

And never, ever, ever . . . lose sight of the differing interests of different constituents:

- Faculty
- Students
- Administration
- Local or regional communities
- Your institution and its culture, history, and traditions
- Consortia (missions, policies, operations)
- Professional organizations

Mistake No. 6

Karen didn't realize that not everyone loves libraries. Instead, she took for granted the notion that everyone—including Paul Andre—would agree that the library is the heart of the university, and would automatically appreciate the value and contribution that libraries make to lives. It seems never to have occurred to her that, in fact, not everyone makes the same assumptions or understands the library's value proposition in the same way. Never, ever, ever . . .

- be surprised to find yourself dealing with successful people who have never—repeat, *never*—used the services of a librarian, and maybe not even of a library, and who will make that clear in no uncertain terms. They honestly don't see library services and resources as valuable, especially in the digital age. It's your job to persuade them. Think very carefully through your own fundamental ideas about the value of libraries. You'll have to articulate them to other people who won't be making the same assumptions.
- kid yourself into believing that "the library" is not *so* over. Your president, provost, and board are probably looking for transformation to keep up with the digital age and the millennial generation. Forget about the notion of a pile of books inside a pile of bricks.
- be surprised to find that your administration expects the library to help pay its own way. Fund-raising, in its many forms, will almost certainly be a major part of your responsibilities.

Mistake No. 7

Karen didn't delegate much responsibility, let alone authority. The plan indicated that she intended to supervise personally the details of expanding access service operations. That would have been expected and appropriate when she was heading up that department. But Karen was now a dean, and we would expect her to have appointed someone else to serve as department head. By supervising the details, Karen would not only be ignoring other responsibilities that belong properly to a dean—she would also completely undermine the authority and effectiveness of the newly appointed department head. Never, ever, ever . . .

- fail to delegate management responsibilities down whenever possible. You *must* develop great managers in order to get your own work done.
- forget that it's the internal team that will handle day-to-day operations, preferably without your direct involvement. Which means that your library's excellence—or lack of it—will be in their hands. The more

they "own" that responsibility, the greater their commitment to doing a truly great job.

- ignore the great good you can do by mentoring other promising people to move into leadership just as you did. Your library, your institution, and your profession will care about the quality of the legacy you leave.

Mistake No. 8

Karen failed to give credit for other people's contributions, and also failed to acknowledge or incorporate board member Paul Andre's input. She presented the library's plan as her own work. (In this case, her actions may have backfired especially badly: not only did the board members not like the plan, they were also under the impression it was entirely the product of Karen's own work.) And when presented with specific points of critique, she heard only the criticism. She was unable to dig deeper or to understand why Paul Andre made the comments he did, or how she might incorporate them into her plan. Never, ever, ever . . .

- neglect to acknowledge and thank everyone who's contributed to whatever it is that you're presenting on their behalf.
- lose sleep over the need to have your name attached to an idea, a plan, a document—whatever. The baggage of self-promotion can really slow you down. To reiterate: you can accomplish a lot if you don't care who gets the credit.[12] But ignore the corollary; don't refuse to acknowledge your own failings and mistakes, quickly and graciously. Apologize— again, quickly and graciously—when it's the right thing to do.

Mistake No. 9

Karen didn't appreciate the beauty of brevity. Instead, her conversation was rambling and unfocused, and her presentation was just too long. Not only were her listeners not riveted, but with the exception of Paul Andre, it appears that they weren't even listening. She didn't understand the substance of the business-oriented questions Paul was asking. Karen presented herself as confused, confusing, and far too scripted. Never, ever, ever . . .

- assume you'll have more than one to two minutes or three to five bullet points to make your case. You really, truly will be dealing with a lot of very busy people.
- stop honing your ability to think on your feet, and to get to the heart of a complicated issue fast. Some of your most crucial communications will be in the form of unscripted dialogues in very public settings. It's

vital to be able to carry on an actual two-sided conversation in these circumstances.

- let your academic correctness get in the way of your ability to understand and use the language of business. Words and phrases that tend to make academics shudder have real value and meaning for many other people. So get comfortable with terms like margin, driver, core business, value proposition, execute, customer, SWOT (strengths, weaknesses, opportunities, and threats), and many, many more.

Mistake No. 10

Karen wouldn't innovate. She presented to the board a plan that appears to have been in every significant respect the same old, same old. In all probability, the board members are actively engaged in a very wide variety of business, charitable, and social activities, and they're likely to be anxious for Acme University to move faster into the twenty-first century—and that probably extends to their expectations for the Acme University library. Never, ever, ever . . .

- stop innovating in order to take advantage of opportunities. This often entails taking risks. Weigh the probable benefits against the probable losses, and against the absolute worst case. But don't be afraid to take a risk.
- be paralyzed by the fear of making a mistake. You're allowed an unlimited number of creative mistakes in life—just don't keep making the same mistake over and over. And be prepared to repair the consequences of your own blunders, to paraphrase Sherlock Holmes.[13] You'll definitely make them. Being able to fix them is the hallmark of a truly creative person.
- hang on too tightly to your inner perfectionist impulses. The world is moving fast, and beta is becoming the normal and expected state for new ideas being introduced. If you're working with a good idea, get a reasonable facsimile of it up and running *fast*—then plan on tweaking as necessary.

ARE YOU AN EFFECTIVE LEADER? HOW DO YOU KNOW?

There's a learning curve involved in making the transition—usually with minimal preparation—from manager to leader. But after you've been in the leadership role for a while, you'll have to be honest with yourself: Are you doing a good job?

How will you know? How will you understand effective leadership? Early in your leadership experience (but not right out of the gate), set benchmarks for yourself in terms of the following:

- Intent
- Strategy
- Execution

And make sure those benchmarks include appropriate feedback from the world beyond yourself—from your staff, your colleagues, your customers, those above you in the hierarchy, and your professional peers.

A key question: Do you like your work? Do you find the leadership experience exhilarating, rewarding, and fun (yes, fun)? Many people are surprised to discover that they don't like this kind of work. If you're among them, look at other options. You may be hurting yourself, your colleagues, your user communities, and your profession by staying in a role that doesn't fit your strengths.

Why would anyone want to be a library leader?

- It's fun—really.
- It unleashes your creativity—really.
- It's rewarding if you get at least some parts of it right.
- And it's tremendously important, especially in this era when librarianship is building bridges from its past into an excitingly different future. If we really, really believe all our own bloviating about the value of libraries and learning, we'd better step up to the plate on our own behalf, and we'd better do it *now*.

NOTES

1. Stephen Covey has developed a series of frameworks for effective leadership that can be found in his many training seminars, presentations, and publications, and in the work of the consulting firm FranklinCovey. These may prove especially useful: http://www.franklincovey.ca/mmedia/pdf/training/Leadership_E.pdf (accessed May 27, 2009) and http://www.franklincovey.com/tc/solutions/leadership-solutions/modular-series-the-4-imperatives-of-great-leaders (accessed May 27, 2009). Among the many works that deal specifically with the processes of change and the leadership that is necessary for effective change, one of the most widely cited and influential is John P. Kotter's *Leading Change* (Boston: Harvard Business School Press, 1996).

2. Neil Postman, *Technopoly: The Surrender of Culture to Technology* (New York: Vintage Books, 1993). This seminal book introduced Postman's thesis that "technology changes everything"—that is, technology does not add or subtract. Instead, it introduces fundamental, transformative change.

3. Joan V. Gallos, "The Dean's Squeeze: The Myths and Realities of Academic Leadership in the Middle," *Academy of Management Learning and Education* 1, no. 2 (2002): 174–84.

4. M. David Dealy, *Change or Die: How to Transform Your Organization from the Inside Out* (Westport, Conn.: Praeger, 2006). According to Dealy (19ff.), the five great change mistakes are (1) underestimating the power of the status quo, (2) favoring consensus over conflict, (3) avoiding risk rather than managing it, (4) only paying lip service to creativity, and (5) failing to encourage change agents.

5. Edward R. Tufte, *The Cognitive Style of PowerPoint* (Cheshire, Conn.: Graphics Press, 2003).

6. The FranklinCovey leadership training seminar employs this comparison. See note 1 above.

7. Stephen Covey's four leadership imperatives: see note 1 above.

8. See note 1.

9. "You can accomplish a lot if you don't care who gets the credit": although this quote is widely attributed to Harry S. Truman or to Ronald Reagan, either of these U.S. presidents would have been paraphrasing. According to *The Columbia World of Quotations* as cited at http://www.bartleby.com/66/45/40245.html (accessed May 27, 2009), the original quotation is attributed to C. E. Montague, British author and journalist (1867–1928), and reads thus: "There is no limit to what a man can do so long as he does not care a straw who gets the credit for it" (Montague, *Disenchantment*, ch. 15, sect. 3, 1922).

10. Roger Fisher, Bruce Patton, and William Ury, *Getting to Yes: Negotiating Agreement without Giving In*, 2nd ed. (New York: Penguin, 1991).

11. William Ury, *The Power of a Positive No: How to Say No and Still Get to Yes* (New York: Bantam Dell, 2007).

12. See note 9.

13. Sir Arthur Conan Doyle, "The Adventure of the Solitary Cyclist," in *Adventures of Sherlock Holmes* (New York: Harper & Brothers, 1930).

Index

About the Editor

Jack Fritts is the director of library services at Benedictine University in Lisle, Illinois. He has been at Benedictine since 2002. On the way to his current position, he managed to avoid some of the errors addressed in this work but also managed to fall headfirst into others. Along the way, he has held many of the jobs that seem to fill the bios of writers, although writing was not his primary aim. Some of those jobs included church cleaner, newspaper stand vendor, dock worker, delivery driver, camp counselor, and sales clerk. Once he got past those, he spent time as a classroom teacher, a school media specialist, and a librarian. He also ventured into the world of consortium management for a spell before settling at Benedictine.

He holds both a Master of Education and a Master of Arts in Library and Information Science, and he finds both degrees useful as he progresses through life. He likes to tell stories and is a firm believer in the philosophy of managing by wandering around. Jack has been an active participant in distance learning library services for over twenty years, and was around during the early discussions that led to the transition from discussion group to section of the body that is now known as the Distance Learning Section (DLS) of the Association of College and Research Libraries (ACRL). He has chaired many committees within DLS and has held most of the elected offices as well. He has also been active in the Library Leadership and Management Association (LLAMA) and the Library and Information Technology Association (LITA), and serves as a mentor in the American Library Association's New Members Round Table (NMRT) mentoring program and in the New Directors Mentoring program.

About the Contributors

Thomas Abbott, Ph.D., dean of libraries and distance learning at the University of Maine at Augusta, has served in a variety of administrative positions at UMA since 1974, with library management as his core responsibility for the last twenty years. His additional assignments have included being acting chief academic officer, developing a continuing education program, managing 600 student remote campus program, chairing the University of Maine System Library Directors' Council, developing an off-campus library services program, developing an undergraduate library services program at a distance, and most recently providing leadership and support for UMA's academic community for distance-learning delivery. Tom also teaches online in UMA's Human Services Program and consults nationally in the areas of accreditation preparation, organizational structure and design, and distance learning, especially in the library arena. He is also an active contributor to ACRL, where he most recently led the CUPA-HR/ACRL academic librarian position description restructuring, which was used successfully in the fall of 2008.

Anne Marie Casey is library director at Embry-Riddle Aeronautical University. Prior to this she was associate dean of libraries at Central Michigan University and served in a variety of leadership and reference positions in academic and public libraries and being the chair of the ACRL Distance Learning Section. As the oldest of four children, Anne Marie learned about management mistakes very early on: by making most of them and having to clean up the mess.

H. Frank Cervone, Ph.D., vice chancellor for information services at Purdue University Calumet, has written numerous articles and five books on topics related to information technology. He also writes a regular column for OCLC Systems and Services, *International Digital Library Perspectives*, and has been an invited speaker at library conferences in the United States, Canada, Great Britain, Australia, and Brazil. He was a member of the NISO working group on metasearch and is the past chair of the CARLI (Consortium of Academic and Research Libraries in Illinois) Learning Objects Task Force. He has a masters in education with a specialization in online teaching and learning from the California State University, a masters in information technology management from DePaul University, and a Ph.D. in management and information systems from Northcentral University.

Connie Costantino, San Jose State University School of Library and Information Science, spent more than 30 years as a school, public, and academic librarian, most recently as library director at Alliant International University (from 1993 to 2003). She also consulted for libraries in Mexico City and Nairobi, Kenya. Dr. Costantino was active in the Association of College and Research Libraries, particularly the Distance Learning Section, and chaired ACRL's International Relations Committee. California colleagues will remember her work as chair of the Mentoring Committee for the California Library Association. Dr. Costantino taught information organizations and management, instructional strategies for information professionals, and international and comparative librarianship at SLIS. Her research focused on information literacy, particularly among undergraduate students and educators.

Luann DeGreve, assistant director for collection services, Benedictine University, is responsible for overseeing all collection services functions including acquisitions, cataloging, collection management, periodicals, government documents, and special collections. Prior to joining Benedictine University, Luann was the interlibrary loan/serials librarian at Quincy University and a junior-high social studies teacher in Indiana. Luann received her bachelors degree in history from Butler University of Wisconsin Stevens Point, her masters in library science from Indiana University, and her masters in history from Purdue University.

Harvey Gover, assistant campus librarian at the Max E. Benitz Memorial Library at Washington State University, Tri-Cities, is a specialist in regional campus library services for land-grant university systems. He is a tenured library faculty member at Washington State University (WSU) Libraries, where he serves as assistant campus librarian, WSU Tri-Cities. Harvey earned his bachelors degree at Baylor University, his masters in library information system from the University of Texas at Austin, and a master of arts in teaching at Tarleton State University, a regional campus of Texas A&M University. He was formerly the public services librarian at Tarleton. Harvey is a widely published, internationally recognized spokesperson for and principal author of the 2008 *Standards for Distance Learning Library Services.* He served as a U.S. department of state speaker and received a specialist grant for travel to India in 2002. He presented at the international conference of the Global Alliance for Transnational Education (GATE) in Paris in September, 2002. He is a past recipient of the ACRL/DLS Haworth Press Conference Sponsorship Award (2008).

Daniel J. Julius, vice president for academic affairs at the University of Alaska System of Higher Education, Fairbanks, began his career as an assistant research librarian at Bernard M. Baruch College, City University of New York. He has subsequently held senior academic positions, including chief academic officer at Benedictine University, the University of San Francisco, the California State University System and Vermont State College System; and faculty member at the University of California–Berkeley, Stanford University, and the University of New Hampshire. Dr. Julius has published widely in the areas of organizational behavior, industrial labor relations, and higher education, has led or served on ten accreditation teams, and has received numerous awards including Fulbright and Kellogg fellowships. He received his degrees from the Ohio State University, Columbia University, and Stanford University.

Michael Lorenzen, head of reference services, Central Michigan University, Mount Pleasant, is the head of reference services at Central Michigan University. He has his MLS from Kent State University, a master's in education from Ohio University, and a doctorate in educational leadership from Central Michigan University. He has published more than twenty-five articles in the library literature over the last fifteen years on a variety of topics, including library management, library instruction, and information literacy. He lives in Mt. Pleasant, Michigan, with his wife and two sons.

Patrick Mahoney, senior information analyst, the Mitre Corporation, McLean, Virginia, has previously performed reference and information learning services to distance students with Central Michigan University's Off-Campus Library Services. He participated in constructing subject tutorials on the university's off-campus website and also conducted classroom sessions on electronic information usage at the university's off-site faculties in the western U.S. He is currently a senior information analyst with the MITRE Corporation, performing research on government performance and accountability and renewable energy initiatives. Patrick holds graduate degrees in business administration and information management, both from Emporia State University.

Kathleen Walsh, dean of the library and interim deputy provost, National-Louis University, Chicago, previously served as dean of the library and interim deputy provost at National-Louis University. Her professional focus in recent years has been on the processes by which one moves from management to leadership.